ETHICS AND PSYCHOLOGY

This highly original book explores the idea and potential of psychology in the context of ethical theory, and the idea of ethics in the context of psychology. In so doing, it not only interrogates how we come to understand ethics and notions of right behaviour, but also questions the discipline of psychology and how it functions in the twenty-first century. Neill turns psychology inside out, controversially suggesting that psychology no longer exists. He proposes a rebirth of psychology based on an intricate and detailed examination of *who* we really are, and how we come to structure this idea of ourselves. Taking the idea of ethics seriously, Neil allows us to see psychology in a totally new light, addressing key points, such as:

- the inadequacy of psychology to address the question of ethics throughout history;
- why thinking through the question of ethics necessarily brings us into confrontation with a question of psychology;
- what we actually do when we do psychology and how, via a serious consideration of ethics, we might do this differently and better.

Ethics and Psychology presents readers with a new understanding of both ethics and psychology which will appeal to anyone active within and critically eng~~~~~~~~~~~~~~ the field.

Dr Calum N where he has taught and untaught currently a lecturer in Critical Ps Edinburgh Napier University.

Concepts for Critical Psychology: Disciplinary Boundaries Rethought

Series editor: Ian Parker

Developments inside psychology that question the history of the discipline and the way it functions in society have led many psychologists to look outside the discipline for new ideas. This series draws on cutting edge critiques from just outside psychology in order to complement and question critical arguments emerging inside. The authors provide new perspectives on subjectivity from disciplinary debates and cultural phenomena adjacent to traditional studies of the individual.

The books in the series are useful for advanced-level undergraduate and postgraduate students, researchers and lecturers in psychology and other related disciplines such as cultural studies, geography, literary theory, philosophy, psychotherapy, social work and sociology.

Published titles

Surviving Identity
Vulnerability and the psychology of recognition
Kenneth McLaughlin

Psychologisation in Times of Globalisation
Jan De Vos

Social Identity in Question
Construction, subjectivity and critique
Parisa Dashtipour

Cultural Ecstasies
Drugs, gender and the social imaginary
Ilana Mountian

Decolonizing Global Mental Health
The psychiatrization of the majority world
China Mills

Self Research
The intersection of therapy and research
Ian Law

The Therapeutic Turn
How psychology altered Western culture
Ole Jacob Madsen

'This remarkable book takes us through different versions of what it might mean to join the question of "ethics" with the assumptions and practices of "psychology". Beginning with some famous studies of ethical behaviour, it rapidly moves into an unconventional and compelling exploration of how the ethical and the psychological might refute and infect each other. *Ethics and Psychology* is surprising, accessible, challenging and vivid and should be read by anyone interested in how psychology functions in the culture of our times.'

Stephen Frosh, Birbeck College, London, UK

'Calum Neill observes psychology closely, via philosophy and its puzzling of the emergence of the self. His argument for ethics shimmers, tightrope across the dark. Edges that claimed to hold psychology and ethics – and keep both apart from poetry – are re-energized as loci of uncertainty. This is a book that will elicit bleats from the technocrats and yips of joy from readers who, like poets, embrace subjectivity as emergence, a move not a statistic, always and productively creative.'

Erin Mouré, Poet and Translator of Poetry, Montreal, Canada

'Psychology has a troubling relationship with "the good" and Calum Neill brings us into this identity conflict in a manner that is both upsetting and inspiring. The interdisciplinary dimension of his text draws the reader along and leaves her without a hiding place from the troubled state of this field.'

David M. Goodman, Associate Dean of Academic Affairs and Student Services, Boston College, Boston, USA

'With rigour and clarity, Calum Neill offers a maverick perspective on what is, or *should be*, psychology's most crucial issue: ethics. From Mill to Nietzsche, Kant to Keats, Neill reminds us that language remains our place of most potential; only through language – its excess, its poiesis – can we confront our subjecthood and write the human psyche.'

Oana Avasilichioaei, Poet and Translator, Montreal, Canada

'I thoroughly enjoyed reading this book. It is written exceptionally well, compelling from the start, and no less so by the accessible, everyday examples the author uses to clarify and amplify rather complicated and dense philosophical concepts and arguments. Yet, for all the ease of comprehension and reading, the author never sacrifices academic and scholarly integrity, and never "dumbs it down", maintaining a rigorous, critical and challenging analysis throughout. This book comes highly recommended.'

Leswin Laubscher, Duquesne University, Pittsburgh, USA

ETHICS AND PSYCHOLOGY

Beyond codes of practice

Calum Neill

Routledge
Taylor & Francis Group

LONDON AND NEW YORK

First published 2016
by Routledge
2 Park Square, Milton Park, Abingdon, Oxon OX14 4RN

and by Routledge
711 Third Avenue, New York, NY 10017

Routledge is an imprint of the Taylor & Francis Group, an informa business

© 2016 Calum Neill

British Library Cataloguing in Publication Data
A catalogue record for this book is available from the British Library

Library of Congress Cataloging in Publication Data
Names: Neill, Calum, 1968– author.
Title: Ethics and psychology: beyond codes of practice / Calum Neill.
Description: New York: Routledge, 2016.
|Series: Concepts for critical psychology | Includes bibliographical references and index.
Identifiers: LCCN 2015042645| ISBN 9780415686709 (hardback: alk. paper) | ISBN 9780415686693 (paperback: alk. paper) | ISBN 9781315625218 (e-book)
Subjects: LCSH: Psychology. | Ethics–Psychological aspects.
Classification: LCC BF47.N45 2016 | DDC 170.1/9–dc23
LC record available at http://lccn.loc.gov/2015042645

ISBN: 978-0-415-68670-9 (hbk)
ISBN: 978-0-415-68669-3 (pbk)
ISBN: 978-1-315-62521-8 (ebk)

Typeset in Bembo
by HWA Text and Data Management, London
Printed in Great Britain by Ashford Colour Press Ltd

For Atticus

CONTENTS

FOREWORD

This is a book for thinking, for reflecting on what we do to other people, and to ourselves in the process, for what happens to us when we treat other people like things instead of as human beings. It has an unusual shape because it is raising fundamental questions about how we come to know about what we are and what we have become as a result of having developed this peculiar discipline we call 'psychology'. Psychologists all too often think they know what they are dealing with in their research, what kind of things they gather together in the experimental laboratories or what kind of 'participants' they enrol in their interview studies when they step outside their laboratories into what they call the 'field'. When psychologists become members of 'ethics committees' they often carry those assumptions with them, and they then explain to 'non-psychologists' how they should and should not treat what were once upon a time called their 'subjects'. Instead of instructing us about what 'ethics' is, this book shows us what it is to struggle ethically with what we know. The book won't subject you to an already pre-formed truth about psychology, but will take you on a journey to reflect on what we are up to as we try and arrive at that truth.

It would be easier, perhaps, to address these kinds of issues if we were sure that we knew, to start with, what human beings actually are. Instead, Calum Neill takes us through a series of complex debates about the nature of subjectivity. You will notice that this 'subjectivity' – and the correlative 'intersubjectivity' that binds us together – is of the nature of a human 'subject' that is very different from the 'subjects' referred to in the old psychology experiments. They were once called subjects, but psychologists who became anxious about 'ethics' noticed that they were really being treated as objects. Whence came the hope that the problem could be tidied up by abandoning the word 'subject' altogether. This book retrieves from philosophical debate a more nuanced and, we could say, respectful notion of the human subject, one which attends to questions of agency and transformation as well as the questions of control and obedience with which the book opens.

The frightful experiments which opened the psychologists' eyes to the role of ethics in research were actually, at the very same time as being a warning about power, a warning about the nature of psychology itself. What *Ethics and Psychology: Beyond Codes of Practice* allows us to think about is the way that the mainstream response to the problem of ethics in psychology – and it is precisely treated as a 'problem' to be solved by most psychologists – was to deal with the restriction on human agency by rushing to put in place many more restrictions. This is exactly the problematic of 'codes of practice'. These so-called ethical procedures are too often codes which actually close down reflection on what we are doing alongside those we are doing things to. We appreciate, as we work our way through the book, how important it is to be doing things 'with' rather than 'to' others. But at the same time we take a distance from what the 'with' is between; we take a distance from our own subjectivity as we reflect on what we are doing in our research, and we take a distance from a simple appeal to 'intersubjectivity' that might seem to solve the problem. Instead we see that we must work 'outwith' others in order to be human subjects. This would be one way of ensuring that new forms of enquiry are oriented to the human subject as one who acts, one who really is a participant in a process where they may learn something and change themselves instead of offering themselves up to the psychologist who will then know more about them, who will then pretend to know more that can be presented in a standard-shaped academic book.

Ian Parker
University of Leicester

1

CONJUNCTIONS

What is the significance in a conjunction? It seems simple enough. Ethics and psychology. And yet, as soon as we assume it as simple, it already takes on a particular meaning. Ethics and psychology, a simple juxtaposition, without essential relation. There is ethics and there is psychology and the two may sit, unproblematically, side by side. But is any such juxtaposition ever so simple, so unproblematic? As soon as two are brought together, is there not then some implication or expectation of a relation, a discourse, a cross-pollination, an infection, a compatibility? And if this compatibility doesn't seem to offer itself, if the fit isn't so neat, the jagged edges of one tearing the other, what then? Do we simply cover it over with a cough and a diverting glance? Or does this conjunction rather imply a temporary encounter, a fleeting meeting, a matter of convenience? This sense of transient coupling would imply that there is nothing intrinsic in the conjunction, one partner in the conjoining might be quite replaceable with another. And, yet, is there not still a stronger sense of conjunction where the 'and' bonds, where one term is properly implied in the other. Ethics and psychology. And is this ever a symmetrical pairing? Can we have an ethics which is not somehow already psychological? Can we have a psychology, or do a psychology, which is not somehow already imbued with ethical questions? But still the 'and' which conjoins also separates. It is then a matter of reading and a matter of reading in which we inevitably, if not always easily or obviously, find ourselves. The conjunction is never simple, only seemingly so. In those three letters, that oh-so-common word we almost don't see, we read the relationship we assume to be there, and in so reading, we find reflected the idea of ourselves we would think to find in, not simply psychology, but ethics too.

2

A FAMILIAR SCENE

It is a familiar scene, perhaps, although one in which few of us have found ourselves. A man is sitting in a room, strapped to a chair with an electrode attached to his wrist. In an adjacent room, another man sits before a machine which is labelled with the words 'Shock Generator'. In a horizontal line, thirty switches are clearly marked with numbers climbing from 15 at one end to 450 at the other. These numbers indicate voltages. Or at least they appear to. The second man has been instructed to read out words from a provided list. The first man should respond with the correct word pair for each word which is read to him. If he does not, the first man is instructed to administer an electric shock by flicking one of the switches before him. Each time a wrong answer is given, the second man should move to a higher voltage. The ruse is that the two men are involved in an experiment designed to investigate the effects of punishment on learning. The scenario, of course, if you have even the briefest familiarity with academic psychology, is Milgram's notorious 'Behavioural Study of Obedience' (1963). Or, if you have less familiarity with academic psychology, the scene is perhaps one you remember from watching Derren Brown's *The Heist* or one of the various other media re-enactments.

Milgram's experiment is one of those you are likely to encounter studying psychology at even the most elementary levels. It is a standard of secondary or high-school courses, such as the 'A' level in England, as well as first-year university psychology courses around the world. It has also, through people like Derren Brown, entered into public consciousness.

The significance of the experiment is manifold. Derren Brown, in his introduction to his restaging of the experiment, describes Milgram's original as speaking 'volumes about the nature of responsibility' (Brown, 2006). Milgram himself is more cautious and seems careful at each turn not to leap to generalise from what are, after all, rather particular circumstances. One curious particularity to which Milgram draws our attention in his original report of the experiment is the location of the experiment within the bounds of psychology. He tells us:

> There is, at best, ambiguity with regard to the prerogatives of a psychologist and the corresponding rights of his subject. There is a vagueness of expectation concerning what a psychologist may require of his subject, and when he is overstepping acceptable limits.
>
> (Milgram, 1963: 377)

Milgram's specificity and Brown's generalisation, put together, say something interesting and important about the place of psychology in the contemporary world and, more particularly, about the relation between psychology and ethics.

Milgram's experiment (or experiments; for he went on to conduct a range of similar experiments, modifying key details such as gender and location) are often held up within psychology as an example from the bad old days before the necessary and necessarily beneficial introduction of codes of practice. Perhaps unfairly, Milgram's experiment is usually lumped in with what is seen as that other great ethical failure in twentieth-century psychology, Zimbardo's Stanford Prison experiment. Zimbardo had sought to explore issues of conformity through role-playing a rudimentary prison scenario wherein male students were assigned either the role of guard or the role of prisoner. The experiment is probably best known for the fact that it soon degenerated into physical and psychological abuse. It is also well-known as something of a model for the abusive behaviours documented as having taken place at the US military prison Abu Ghraib. The textbook pairing of Milgram's and Zimbardo's experiments makes some sense insofar as both sought to uncover something of man's (both experiments were originally focused on male subjects) ethical limits in the face of authority (Haney et al. 1973). They appear, however, quite different in terms of the care with which they were executed. As is well-documented, Zimbardo's experiment was allowed to spiral out of control to the extent that it was considered, by Zimbardo's own fiancée, that human rights abuses were taking place. By comparison, the Milgram experiment appears to be a much more gentle affair. The participants are duped, of course, but no one is actually electrocuted. No real harm is done. Unless, that is, one considers the psychological harm of being made to think that you are the kind of person who would administer a lethal electric shock simply because a man in a white coat told you to. Read in this way, we can perhaps see that the two experiments function slightly differently in relation to the codes of practice which were forged in their wake. The Zimbardo experiment appears to alert us to the fact that we need to be protected from psychologists. The Milgram experiment perhaps then tells us that we need to be protected from psychology itself.

This returns us to the opposition between Derren Brown's claim that the Milgram experiment tells us something profound about the nature of responsibility and Milgram's own caution in claiming much at all beyond the confines of his own experiment. Milgram is clearly the more scientific and understands the pitfalls of overhasty generalisation. As is evident from his later variations on the experiment, he was sensitive to scientific standards, such as ecological and external validity. Brown's broader claim, however, points towards the fact that whether or not one exercises delicate caution in one's claims, such claims can and will be made nonetheless. Milgram's experiment has entered into public consciousness, it has become a part of twentieth-century folklore and, so elevated, it now appears to tell us something indelible and true about human nature. Few people, in the grand scheme of things, even those studying and even those teaching and producing psychology, will actually have read Milgram's report or the lengthier and more in-depth version that is his 1974 monograph, *Obedience to Authority*. But this does not stop a particular perspective on human capability emerging on the basis of this source and its now numerous tributaries. This ought to draw us to another crucial relation between psychology and ethics.

Where the kinds of codes of practice which have emerged since the 1960s seek to ensure that psychology, both in terms of research and clinical practice, is conducted in such a way that it is seen to be ethically justifiable, there is another side to this which necessarily escapes any such code of practice and that is the ethics of the persistence of psychology itself. As is evident in the reception of the Milgram experiment, psychology speaks. It has effects and these effects, given the position psychology holds in our society, sclerose into truths. Milgram, in seeking to explore obedience to authority, seemed sensitive to the fact that psychologists were suitable examples of such authority figures. What resounds from the reception of his work is that it is psychology itself as a haunting, dominant, omnipresence in twenty-first-century life which has become the authority. The reach of psychology is such that it infects and colours every aspect of our lives. Wherever you go, by dint of the fact that you go there, there is psychology. This is not because psychology simply is an integral part of who and what we are. Rather, it is because psychology has become the default way in which we conceive of ourselves. This way of thinking ourselves has become so naturalised, so unquestioned, that not only are we largely unaware of it but, more than this, the very suggestion that there is another way of thinking ourselves can seem implausible, convoluted and perhaps even rather threatening.

We only need to remind ourselves that the discipline of psychology, which seems so integral to contemporary life, was only born in the late nineteenth century. The very word 'psychology' was only introduced into the English language in the late seventeenth century, having first appeared in its Latin form in the late fifteenth or early sixteenth century as the apparent title of a now lost manuscript by the Croatian poet Marko Marulic (Krstic, 1964). As preposterous as it may seem to claim that contemporary psychology is only a particular way of conceiving human being, it is surely more preposterous to suggest that there would be a seamless continuum in how we conceive ourselves between the before and the after of the invention of psychology.

Psychology enjoys a rather peculiar position in comparison to most other disciplines of study insofar as it consists in an epistemological loop. The object of psychology and the agent hoping to explore that object are categorically the same. Whatever truths psychologists uncover or posit as to the mind and behaviour of human beings, there is no escaping the fact that they themselves are one of the category they would seek to explain. This categorical equivalence isn't a simple matter of the organic but, more complexly, the loop or the obstacle consists in the fact that the thought that the psychologist would pursue to uncover the thought or thought processes as the object of study and the thought which would seek to explain this thought are all, necessarily, of the same category and thus subject to the same critique. There is no outside. Where it is generally accepted that true objectivity is an epistemological impossibility, this unobtainability is taken to an extreme in psychology, to the point where claims to objectivity would have to be rightly considered absurd. Added to this, the broad aims of most academic psychology – to tell us something definite about expansive sections of human populations through the generalisation of apparent findings to absent and presumably quite different people on the basis of projected probabilities – necessarily ignores the inconvenient fact that you cannot determine probability on the basis of an incomplete set.

Most troublesome, however, for the viability of psychology is an internal uncertainty as to its proper object. As an academic discipline, psychology has had enormous success. This success notwithstanding, it is beset by what we might, in a psychological idiom, term an identity crisis. Psychology wants to be a science. It gazes up at its disciplinary neighbours in the hard sciences and aches for the status they enjoy. If psychology could attain the status of a science, this would elevate it onto a higher platform. It would be taken more seriously. Its findings might take on the value of truths, of certainties. And it might enjoy greater governmental, financial and perhaps even public support. To achieve this slide down the corridor to the science faculty, psychology had to posture as a science. It has increasingly, over the twentieth and into the twenty-first century, adopted the scientific method and scientific rhetoric and has increasingly concerned itself with quantitative measurement. For this posturing or realignment to work, psychology has had to become a more empirical discipline. The problem here is as glaring as it is foreclosed. What seems the obvious object of psychology is not an empirical phenomenon. The *psyche*, the mind, the thing that psychology once claimed to study, isn't an extended thing, isn't something we can access and measure. This has led many psychologists to edge ever closer to their cousins in the neurosciences and to increasingly focus their attention on the brain instead. Not only does this inevitably and rather obviously have an effect on what psychology is but, much more devastatingly for psychology, it cannot but, ultimately, be a form of disciplinary suicide as psychology becomes either absorbed into or eclipsed by the neurosciences. From one perspective this is all well and good. Understood in an evolutionary framework, we might simply say that psychology has become obsolete. We should, however, perhaps ask, what is lost in this process? Somewhere along the line, the question of the *psyche*, the mind, has inevitably dropped out of the picture. If psychology is intent on abandoning its own proper object of study and melding into its preferred neighbour, then what, if anything, is going to pick up where psychology left off?

This identity crisis is, of course, going to impact on the practice of psychology, and in various obvious ways. Amongst these we ought to count ethics. You could even say that the questions of what it is that psychology thinks it is and what is potentially lost in its contemporary yearning for scientific status are already ethical questions, perhaps even touching on very core of what ethics might mean or the very possibility of ethics. Understood in this way, the abandonment of its proper object of study could already be understood as not only the death knell of psychology but, arguably more significantly, the refusal of ethics itself.

And yet psychology appears to position itself in such a way that it might, more than any other discipline, tell us something meaningful about human interaction and, in so doing, it appears to appoint itself as the expert with regards to applied, and therefore, apparently, genuinely meaningful ethics.

When, in 1964, a young woman by the name of Kitty Genovese was attacked and murdered in a populated area of New York, the idea that there might be something wrong with 'us' and our moral sensibility captured the public imagination. *The New York Times* reported that 'For more than half an hour thirty-eight respectable, law-abiding citizens in Queens watched a killer stalk and stab a woman in three separate attacks in Kew Gardens' (Gansberg, 1964). The report goes on to emphasise how not one of the thirty-eight bystanders telephoned the police during the incident and only one did so afterwards. That the newspaper report turned out to be somewhat inaccurate did not stop a huge question-mark looming over our supposedly innate humanity. How, people began to ask, was it possible for witnesses to do nothing when someone was so obviously in need of help. Social psychologists quickly rose to the challenge of exploring this phenomenon.

This wasn't, of course, the first time that psychology had stepped into the fray. As we have already discussed, a few years earlier Milgram had sought to explore a different doubt with regard to our innate moral tendencies. This was some twenty years after the Holocaust in Europe. Many people seemed to understand, or want to understand, the Holocaust as a German problem. What was it about German culture or the German people which could allow them to engage in acts of genocide? As if they were the only ones. A few months before Milgram's initial experiment, Adolf Eichmann had famously stood trial for his part in the Holocaust. As transportation administrator during the Final Solution, Eichmann's job entailed determining the logistics of the extermination of the Jews of Europe. His famous defence was that he was only following orders. Milgram set out to see if such a mindset of deferring the responsibility for one's harmful actions was more widespread than imagined. He devised an experiment to test whether ordinary Americans would inflict pain on another ordinary American, and, if so, how much pain they would inflict. That is to say, he wanted to see the extent to which people would inflict harm on each other simply because they were told to do so.

Between Milgram's experiments and the rash of experiments which were conducted in the wake of the Kitty Genovese case, a range of ethical questions are raised. Many of the post-Genovese studies claimed to demonstrate a phenomenon which has come to be known as the 'bystander effect' (Darley and Latané, 1968). The bystander effect is the name given to the perceived social phenomenon whereby people will witness a situation in which a person is or people are clearly in need of some sort of assistance and yet they, the witnesses, do not help. That is, they stand, or perhaps more often walk on, by. Darley and Latané were among the first to construct experiments which sought to demonstrate and explore the phenomenon and were followed by many others. The psychological world became so concerned with this particular mode of not helping that it appears to have over-shadowed all other forms of potentially ethical behavior. People would feign seizures (Darley and Latané, 1968), collapse on subways (Piliavin, Rodin and Piliavin, 1969), cry out from adjacent rooms (Latané and Rodin, 1969) and the psychologists would measure the responses, or lack thereof. The overwhelming conclusion was that people will tend not to help in many circumstances, such as when there is an apparent socially acceptable excuse or reason not to or when they are not physically present with the victim. Many of the studies seemed to suggest an inverse relation between group size and propensity to help and came to focus more positively on the conditions under which help would be provided rather than the bare fact that it often wasn't.

This wave of experiments, which continues to dominate the study of what has come to be known as pro-social behaviour today, tells an interesting story about how psychology perceives humanity and ethics. The first observation which should be pointed out is that few, if any, of the reports of these studies make any explicit reference to ethics. Rather, the literature tends to refer to 'norms', the provision of 'aid' or 'help' and 'emergencies'. The implication here, then, is that what would constitute 'help' or socially desirable behaviour is already determined and delimited in advance. Few would dispute that, when the participants hear a man apparently having a seizure, the socially upright thing to do would be to move to his assistance. This is, however, at best a rather thin example of ethical behaviour. There is no suggestion here that the authors of these reports would dismiss other forms of what might be considered ethical behaviour and the very fact that the term 'ethics' tends to be absent from the write-ups could be understood as supporting the idea that the concern of these studies is intentionally focused and not exclusive. Nonetheless, the overwhelming focus on this type of behaviour should also be understood in the context of the complex mirroring between psychology and lived life. The focus of the studies tends to be on a particular form or mode of behaviour and, in singling this out, the discipline of psychology at one and the same time suggests that this is what is already deemed important and reflects this selected mode of behaviour as what ought to be important. In so focusing on one particular conception of socially positive or potentially ethical behaviour, without commenting on others, the effect is to allow those others to conceptually recede.

The mode of behaviour explored here is socially visible, individual, reactive and, crucially, somewhat artificial. It perhaps makes sense to start with the last of these. Psychology, and social psychology in particular, is often criticised for lacking in ecological validity. When experiments are constructed to explore particular perceived or conceived phenomenon, there is a tendency to perform the experiment in restricted conditions where variables can be more easily controlled and monitored. Again, the pretentions to scientific status. Even when the experiment is not carried out in the cosy confines of a university psychology laboratory, it is generally considered necessary to factor out confounding variables. For example, when Piliavin and her co-researchers sought to address the problem of poor ecological validity in helping behaviour studies, they staged their experiment on a subway train, which they referred to as their laboratory on wheels. The simple issue here is that studies which claim to demonstrate some generalisable truth about human behaviour or nature cannot very well do so when the study is conducted in an unrepresentative setting. The term 'ecological' in *ecological validity* takes its stem from the Greek *oikos* meaning home or habitation. Few of us feel sufficiently at home in a laboratory for that to be considered in anyway a natural setting and, therefore, it can be assumed that our reactions in that context cannot necessarily be generalised to any other. This is without moving to consider other confounding contexts such as the fact of being aware you are partaking in an experiment, even if, as is usually the case, you don't know what that experiment is really about or the fact that you are with strangers. The simple relocation to a non-laboratory setting clearly doesn't really address the underlying problem here. While Piliavin and colleagues did succeed in constructing an experiment in a non-artificial setting, the results still could never be generalised beyond the rather narrow context of a New York subway with all the interrelating factors specific to that context. Added to this, in their endeavour to be good experimentalists and restrict variations, they chose to stage each iteration of their feigned collapsing passenger on the same route. This most likely increases the possibility of passengers experiencing the odd sensation of *déjà vu* as they witness the same man collapsing again in the same manner in the same place.

As well as raising questions as to the value of the research, there is a double instance of deception at work in many experimental studies. On a first level, there is most often an element of deception at work in the studies themselves. Participants are usually told that they are present to take part in a study which is concerned with something other than the true object of investigation. Participants in the Darley and Latané study referred to above were told they were to take part in a discussion about personal problems associated with college life. Participants in the Milgram study thought they were testing a teaching technique. While the Piliavin study sidesteps the most obvious mode of deception here, in that the 'participants' are not explicitly lied to concerning the nature of the study, they are still rather obviously deceived insofar as they are supposed to believe that the confederate collapsing before them is for real. On a second and much more slippery level, there is an often ignored dimension of deception in that the implication tends to be that the results of the study say something meaningful about people in general.

The very promulgation of findings has the effect of creating a particular idea of what people do, what people are like and what counts as normal. This in itself is already an ethical issue. It is clearly something of a stretch to take the narrow information gathered in relation to one particular collection of individuals at one particular moment in time and project this onto other individuals in different contexts and different times. As the information from studies is diluted and re-presented in other articles, textbooks and the wider media, this becomes a greater problem. An artificial picture of humanity is drawn and this artificial picture is then circulated and consumed. We see ourselves in what we are told, whether we were there in the first place or not. In this way what is disseminated and digested becomes a part of the very thing to be explored in the first place. Psychology, in this sense, is never a neutral science. Numerous complex ethical issues arise through the very conduct of psychology and the decisions which have been made to conduct it, and confine its conduct, in particular ways. It would seem that a particular ethical responsibility perhaps then goes along with psychology's peculiar status and peculiar way of positing itself.

3

CULTURE

In a quotidian sense, ethics in, or ethics relating to, psychology can be understood as a question of how we ought to proceed when conducting this thing we call psychology. In terms of researching psychology, then, this would mean that ethics concerns how we go about doing our research. Ethical theory in a broader sense often covers much more than this. Ethics, in the history of philosophy, has been located not only in terms of action but also in terms of character. In fact, the term 'ethics' actually or etymologically refers to character, deriving as it does from the Greek *ethos*. It is in this sense that much ancient Greek philosophy understands ethics as a question of character or virtue, as a question of how one lives one's life on a daily basis. When it comes to the practice of ethics in psychology, such a notion of character appears to have been lost. When one talks of ethics in relation to psychology, one is most usually referring to either research ethics or the ethics of clinical practice. As different as these might both be, and as different as the questions and considerations they might raise might be, both locate ethics within a delimited practice. They then emphatically point to what they call *codes of practice* as the measures of ethics.

As obvious as it might seem, talk of ethics in psychology is not only delimited to practice (as opposed to character) but it is also delimited to certain aspects of practice. Codes of ethical practice tend not to indicate what, for example, one ought to wear when conducting one's research. While it is conceivable that certain articles of clothing or their absence could be understood to cause offence and thus might raise certain ethical issues, the choice to wear, for example, a Hawaiian shirt with matching tie would, as offensive as that might be to the participants' sense of taste, not usually be construed as constituting an ethical concern. We might argue that wearing something like this is inappropriate but we would probably not argue that it is unethical. This is to make the obvious point that ethics would normally be understood to be limited to matters relating to the benefit or harm of others. It is also already, however, to problematise this seemingly uncontentious assumption, insofar as we seem to be suggesting that some degrees of harm, such as the aesthetic, are legitimately separated off here. While this might seem obvious enough, it does raise the important question of when harm is harm. Or, to phrase this in the seemingly more trivial formulation, when is taste just taste? It is to raise, that is, the question of value. And value, lest we forget, is an attributed quality.

If an ethical position or claim can be grounded in or through an appeal to something outside of itself, then it can be understood to be in some way absolute. If, for example, one believes in a particular idea of God and a particular idea of God's will, then one is likely to ground one's idea of ethics in this idea of what God wants or decrees. One might believe, for example, that, once upon a time, God gave a selected member of the community a set of stone tablets containing the basic tenets of a moral code. Something like the Ten Commandments, from within the Judeo-Christian belief system, becomes an inviolable prescription. There is no questioning it. But, then, equally, from the outside it holds no necessary value. To a member of the community of believers, there is, for example, no need to seek any justification for the commandment not to covet or desire your neighbour's house. It is not a question of reason or argument. It is, within the community of belief, a simple moral fact. This is what you ought to do; you ought not to covet your neighbour's house. To the world outside, the situation is not the same. Without the appeal to God and God's will, a vacuum of reason opens up and one necessarily finds oneself asking, why? Why should I not covet my neighbour's house? What harm is there in it? And even if there is some harm in it, why does this make it wrong? Many groups adhere to very particular prohibitions regarding food, from the Roman Catholic prohibition against eating meat on Fridays, to the Islamic and Judaic prohibition against eating pork, to the Discordian prohibition against eating hot dog sausages in buns. Such prohibitions are hard to grasp from the outside and even when they can be traced back to an apparent logical or practical original ground, this only highlights the apparent groundlessness of current adherence.

Two positions then open up here; an inside and an outside. From the inside of a particular belief system, a certain moral or ethical perspective is set in stone. From outside of this belief system, the same moral perspective is groundless and, therefore, valueless. For the insider, the prescription must be followed. For the outsider, there is simply no such imperative. Such reasoning seems, in our post-Enlightenment world, to be fairly obvious. From this perspective, ethics becomes relative. What is right for one person is wrong for another and vice versa. This, then, returns us to the question of taste. If right for one is wrong for another and there are then no absolutes, what is really to distinguish questions of right and wrong in a moral sense, from questions of right and wrong in an aesthetic or gastronomic sense? I like tea, you like coffee. You like your hot dog in a bun, I prefer it without. You like Bach, I like Beyoncé. I support capital punishment, you don't. What difference does it make?

The obvious difference it makes is that certain of these opinions or perspectives or preferences are likely to come into conflict with each other. When I advocate capital punishment, I am advocating it for society, not for myself. If I advocate it for society, this clearly conflicts with your opposition to it (for society). Arguably, this is one dimension on which ethical issues might be separated out from issues of taste. When I say that I like Beyoncé's music, I am presumably saying that I like listening to Beyoncé, not that I think everybody should be made to listen to Beyoncé's music on public tannoy systems at set hours of each day. Were I suggesting this, then my proposal would start to raise ethical questions. As long as it remains a matter of personal listening pleasure, one might argue that this is a purely private matter which ought not to concern anyone else. Assuming we are not disturbing anyone else, I can listen to Beyoncé as much as I like, you can listen to Bach as much as you like and we can happily agree to disagree as to their aesthetic merits while we tolerate each other's tastes.

Herein lies the rub. Even on the question of musical preferences, the matter is resolved by appeal to tolerance; i.e. through appeal to an ethical position. When what is at stake entails seemingly more significant issues, such as questions of freedom, duty or responsibility, then it is much more difficult to apply a levelling balm of tolerance. Turning back to the question of capital punishment, for example, it seems difficult to sincerely endorse a notion of tolerance in such a debate. One could, of course, argue that we can tolerate another nation operating a system of capital punishment while refusing such a system in our own nation but this in itself only raises further questions in the domain of ethics.

The issue of tolerance brings into relief a core and, arguably, insurmountable problem with what is known as moral relativism. This is the assumption that we can somehow stand outside an ethical question. That is to say, the position of relativism assumes that it is possible to occupy a neutral third position. The problem is that there is no neutral third position. Of course, if we are talking about one particular belief system and another particular belief system, then it is perfectly plausible to assume a third system which is neither of the first two. But that is not the case here. Either one is in the belief system or one is not. Either one endorses a particular ethical position or one does not. Taking the concrete example used above of the Decalogue, either one endorses the Ten Commandments or one doesn't. There is simply no other, third, position available. That is to say, the aloof position which purports an equality in relative moral positions is a myth, a purely imaginary position. If you oppose capital punishment on the grounds that it is wrong to take someone else's life, regardless of what they have done, then it simply makes no logical sense to simultaneously argue that it is acceptable for people from another country to do this because they have a different system or tradition or morality. One perspective contradicts the other. To invoke a supervening requirement of tolerance is simply to move the argument to another question. Now it becomes a question of whether we consider it ethically necessary to endorse tolerance of others' practices and, crucially, to what extent and into which domains we think or feel we can extend this tolerance. Ultimately this line of reasoning will run up against the question of the tolerance of intolerance.

If moral or ethical relativism is demonstrated to be, ultimately, a fiction, or, at best, a variant on taste, where then does this leave the question of ethics? Is it really feasible to claim that ethics is necessarily universal. And, if so, then what might be the content of such an ethics? How might it be possible, that is, to formulate an ethical position or framework which is neither reducible to the fiction of relativism nor simply the imposition of a particular moral perspective. Is there the possibility of a universalism which is not simply a universalised particularism? If not, then we are, effectively, returned to the same problem faced by the relativists. When the chips are down, my morality is the right one and anything else is wrong.

In the context of something like the discipline of psychology, this would be to impose a particular cultural view on other cultures, a move which cannot but help shape the supposed universal claims of the discipline into unreflexive projections through the prism of particular cultural values.

4
NATURE

If ethics can no longer be grounded in an appeal to God or tradition, then does this effectively close down the possibility of ethics per se. If ethics needs to be grounded in something, and cultural conviction only gives rise to a relativism which necessarily encounters an unanswerable agonism at its own borders, and the hypothesis of a natural moral sensibility effectively avoids the question of the ethical entirely, then what remains as a potential ground? What remains to save the possibility of ethics? The traditional answers would have been God or gods. This, as already implied, now seems an untenable answer. Without the presumption of a universal belief in a particular god or set of gods, any such appeal simply collapses into the same problem as any other cultural relativism. Your moral prescriptions may be fine for you and your god but they lack any foundation for me with my god. This is one way of understanding the sense of Nietzsche's statement in *The Gay Science* (2002 [1882]) when he declares that God is dead. Where we might imagine a time and place, such as medieval Europe, in which it would have been uncountenanceable to question the existence of God, it is now common to encounter those who openly disbelieve. This is not merely a point about the demographic extent of religious belief, that less people believe now than then. The point is rather an internal one about the belief itself. The acceptability of atheism or disbelief, as well as surface-level interreligious, and interdenominational, tolerance, cannot but effect a shift in belief itself. My belief in God necessarily loses something of its absolute character when I can happily accept, and even respect, my neighbour's atheistic position. Multiculture appears to force me either into a position of being somewhat disingenuous with my neighbour, insofar as I openly express my toleration of his or her beliefs while privately regarding them as unenlightened, mistaken, Godless, heretical, blasphemous ... or, on the other hand, it puts me into a position of being disingenuous with myself and my God, insofar as I attempt to harbour at one and the same time an unfailing fidelity to a divine being and Its decrees, and an acceptance of Its non-existence and the relative or dubious nature of the decrees attributed to Its name. This is what we might properly understand as the effect of the death of God. It is not simply that it is now acceptable to not believe but, more significantly, that this acceptance has had to become an, albeit contradictory, element of the belief itself. Where it is not, we deem it fundamentalist.

Without something or someone to guarantee our ethico-moral position, is there any possibility of retaining or any sense in attempting to retain any sense of ethics at all? Perhaps it is simply more true to suggest that there are simply functional rules which can be determined in multifarious ways and enforced through the rule of law. Perhaps might or number are right, not because either is intrinsically right but simply because of the power of enforcement that they make possible. Which is to say, we may need order but do we actually need ethics? And yet, there always remains the sense that we *know* the difference between right and wrong and that sometimes might and majority are not held to be on the side of the right.

While the possibility of refusing rule by the majority or the mighty can easily be attributed to adherence to alternative values supported by minority cultural or religious perspectives, this focuses the question misleadingly on external conflict. Focusing instead on the interior of a culture or people, if a sense of the ethical cannot be legitimately derived from a deity or from law, then from what could it be derived? One argument here might be that ethics is somehow natural or organic in origin. With the neurological turn in psychology, this idea must seem essentially appealing. We all, we might argue, know the difference between right and wrong. We may not always act on this knowledge, may not always do the right thing. But we know what the right thing to do would be. This commonplace observation raises interesting questions regarding the consistency between our thoughts, feelings and actions, between our sociality and our selfishness. But it raises much more crucial and, arguably, deeper questions about our relation to notions of right and wrong. *We all know the difference between right and wrong.* But who is *we* here? What happens to those who appear not to know the difference between right and wrong? Are they no longer a part of the group that counts as *we*? Implicit here is the idea that *we all know the difference between right and wrong and those who don't are wrong.* The meaning of *wrong* here starts to wobble slightly. They may be wrong because they are simply bad people or they may be wrong in the sense that they are mistaken or in the sense that there is something *wrong* with them; they are deficient or need to be fixed in some way. The slide here from inherently wrong, in the sense of something like evil, to wrong in the sense of abnormal could itself be understood as demonstrative of the slide from a religious understanding to a psychological understanding, where the latter merely comes to replace the former, leaving much of the assumptions which would underpin the judgement intact. A good illustration of this might be the juxtaposition of Richard Donner's 1976 film *The Omen* and Lynne Ramsay's 2011 film *We Need to Talk About Kevin*. Obvious details aside, the two films essentially tell the same story, that of the birth and subsequent devastation wreaked by a 'deviant' boy. The key difference between the two films is that while *The Omen* attributes the boy's deviance to his Satanic nature, *We Need to Talk About Kevin* suggests the boy's issues arise from his problematic attachment with his mother. Ramsay's film is effectively a remake of Donner's with the necessary update to the contemporary mode of explanation or grand narrative. Evil has a new description but, however superficially tamed it may appear, it walks with the same gait.

Implicit too in the assumption that we all know the difference between right and wrong is the idea of an already existing *right* and *wrong* that we can know. This would be to say that *right* and *wrong* are somehow natural states or categories. At the very least this is conveniently consistent with the implication that there is something *wrong* with people like Kevin who do not understand or adhere to the difference. A natural distinction is one which would be available, naturally, to us all. Again, those who are not endowed with the ability to distinguish are, by definition, deficient. But the notion of a natural morality raises further questions too.

If morality is a natural feature, then would we not expect to find the same morals arising across cultures, across eras and even, perhaps, across species? It is rather obvious, though, that different cultures uphold different ideas and different ideals. What is deemed acceptable in one culture is not necessarily deemed acceptable in another. We behave differently, we have different expectations and we judge differently. Similarly, our standards and social mores differ vastly over time. And, few people seriously expect the same moral standards from an animal as from a human being. This in itself, however, does not really adequately address the question of the natural status, or not, of our moral sense. Leaving aside animals for the time being, the different values or mores upheld by different cultures or traditions could be understood as different implementations of the same root value. One culture may deem it immoral for a man in his twenties to have sex with a seventeen-year-old, while another culture would find this acceptable but would strongly disapprove of the same man having sex with a twelve-year-old. This does not necessarily, however, indicate a different root morality. Both cultures could be understood as upholding the value that mature consent is a prerequisite for sex, but may simply disagree as to what age one has to be in order to count as being able to exercise such mature consent. Such a disparity, while clearly significant in practice, does not necessarily contradict the idea that *we all know the difference between right and wrong*. We might well all innately *know* that it is wrong to take advantage of a minor whilst also acknowledging that the definition of a minor varies from culture to culture.

But even here, buried in this overly simplified example, is a difficult knot. Notions of acceptable ages of consent imply an idea of responsibility. Not only do they indicate that the minor in question is not deemed capable of being responsible for their own actions, they suggest that the adult in question, and the wider community too, is somehow responsible for the child's welfare. This, clearly, is already a moral position. From within the culture in question, such a paternalism may seem quite obviously necessary or, at the risk of being tautological, obviously morally correct. However, from a position outside of the culture in question, quite the opposite perspective may be held. What for one culture may be seen as necessary protection may, for another, be seen as domineering restriction. The point here is not simply that one person's or culture's protection is another's restriction. The deeper point is that the very ability to engage in moral decisions is at stake. We all know the difference between right and wrong but some don't know this yet and therefore have to be protected. While few of us would disagree with this idea on principle, the choice as to where to draw the line and thus who is considered morally capable (and culpable), and who is not, still needs to be made.

Even if we were to concede that moral sense is an innate attribute, the implementation of a natural morality still involves a decision. We might compare this to other senses we would consider quite natural. Just as we have a natural sense of hot and cold, we might argue, so we have a natural sense of right and wrong. The fact that you like it a little hotter than me or that what I consider unpleasantly hot you consider pleasantly warm doesn't mean we don't have the same basic sense mechanism at work. If we are sharing a home, however, we might need to achieve a consensus on what is acceptable. Similarly, then, even if an innate moral sensibility were to exist, and this might for good reason seem unlikely, the outcome or concrete details of such a sensibility are still open to debate.

Added to this, the very rules of the debate themselves are open to debate. What is the right (or wrong) way to decide what is right or wrong? Some would argue that consensus is necessary. Others would hold onto the notion of some sort of self-evident or sovereign standard. Where consensus is sought, again the question arises as to who is included in such a consensus. This immediately raises the following question: who decides who is included in the consensus? Are all opinions, perspectives and arguments equally valid? And what happens when some don't understand the opinions, perspectives and arguments of others? In many ways the notion of sovereign standard is a much simpler one. There simply is a *right* and a *wrong* and these will be revealed to certain amongst us. The obvious problem with this approach is that, when push comes to shove, *we* are generally right and *they* are generally wrong.

The notion of an innate morality or even moral sense falters on a more devastating and ultimately irrefutable logical hurdle. Let's take the simple idea of a natural empathy as the gateway to an innate moral sense. Whether or not an emotional connectivity can be pinpointed and experimentally demonstrated, and many psychologists claim to have done just this, there remains an insurmountable gap between such apparently measurable behaviour and a moral sense. However reliably the average participant in a psychological study responds when faced with another person's distress, that such a display of what might be called empathy is an indicator of a moral sense is a case of putting the cart before the horse. We might well argue that empathy exists as the ground for certain behaviours, but such an argument in no way demonstrates that such behaviours have any moral worth. We would have to have had already demonstrated (or assumed) that the empathetic behaviour in question itself had a moral value which would necessitate already having decided what counts as right or wrong. The argument, quite simply, takes us nowhere.

Imagine a scenario where empathetic arousal might be said to indicate an innate moral tendency. A man is walking by a river and sees a small child fall into the turbulent water. He experiences arousal in his noradrenergic system, causing the projection of neurons to his posterior cortex. In his heightened state of alertness, and the corresponding increase in adrenaline in his system, he moves quickly to dive into the water and rescue the drowning child.

While we can break the experience here down into discrete moments, two important points need to be acknowledged concerning our analysis. First, the breaking down of the experience into moments is already a fitting of the experience into a certain framework of understanding, one which entails not only the selection of what are judged to be relevant elements, the emphasising of particular moments, but also the relation between elements and, crucially, a sense of what the elements might signify. The analysis is, from the very beginning, a selection and an interpretation. It is also then, on a number of levels, an occlusion. It occludes elements which might otherwise have been included, it occludes certain potential meanings which may otherwise have been read into the situation and it occludes other chronologies or causal/influential relations.

Into this already problematic partitioning of experience, we then need to insert what we might call the ethical moment. If our task is to unveil a natural, neurological ethical tendency, then we would need to isolate the point or collaboration of points which would render the experience one which could be described as ethical or in which this ethical tendency could be seen to manifest.

Does the ethical moment of this experience consist in the fact of arousal? Insofar as we might distinguish the actor in our example from other witnesses who were not (or were less) aroused, this might make sense. To locate the ethical here, however, would seem to point to an ethics without responsibility. The actor in a strong sense is determined by the activity we are naming ethical here (the neurological activity) rather than determinant of the action we might call ethical (the saving of the child). Of course, if we wanted to make the argument that we are biologically predisposed to an ethics, this might make perfect sense, but it does seem to reduce ethics to an element in a premobilised chain of events and thus divests it of certain elements we might have considered central to what makes ethics ethics, possibly most crucially, the element of choice or decision.

This leads us to an alternative to the above, wherein we might locate the ethical in the response the actor has to the neurological arousal rather than the neurological arousal itself. In this weaker reading, from the perspective of establishing a hardwired ethics, the brain arousal functions as the necessary pre-requisite for ethical action but surrenders the ethical moment itself to the decision how or whether to respond. There are even arguments from a neurological perspective which suggest that the decision, the neurological activity associated with the decision, occur after the action which would be conventionally understood as the outcome of the decision. From this perspective, it would be difficult to see how the decision itself could be understood to be the ethical moment (in any conventional sense) insofar as it implies a retrospective logic.

The complexities of decision making aside, in each of the possible readings of the hero/drowning child scenario, we encounter a logical problem. In order to consider the grounds of the ethical moment in the scenario, we are necessarily ascribing a value to the action. Somewhere along the line, as the readers of the scenario we need to posit one element as being ethical. The impulse to save a drowning child, the act of saving a drowning child, the neuro-activity experienced in witnessing a drowning child ... we need to have already assigned a value to one of these elements before we might consider it ethical. It is difficult to then see in what sense this points to an innate, natural or biological ethics. What it does, rather, is allow us to appreciate the core mechanism of judgement at work here and the consequent logical separation of instinctual reaction and human values. This then helps to draw us away from the pernicious perspective that we, as a species, are endowed with an innate moral sensibility. Such an assumption appears to rest either upon an equation of the natural with what is not conscious or the equation of what is done or commonly done with what is right. The slippery slope of this appeal to nature lands us in the assumption that, if our distinction between *right* and *wrong* is innate, then there is no real need for any debate at all. People must already be thinking and behaving in a morally upright manner. Either that or there is something wrong with us. Or more worrying, either that or there is something wrong with *them*.

5

CONSEQUENCES

It seems then that the idea of attaining a singular or universal ethics is somewhat out of reach. The attempt to ground ethics in nature appears to merely return us to the basic question of how we might determine what is considered right in the first place. The attempt to ground it in some other external guarantor locks into a more complex question of allegiance, exclusion and, ultimately, a rather similar question of epistemology. The apparent irresolvabilities here are, of course, well documented in the long history of writing on ethics. This history is characterised by a number of quite different approaches. These approaches shape the manner in which we consider ethical questions and thus determine the outcome, or at least the scope of the outcome, of any ethical deliberation into which we enter. More than this, the approach we take to the question of ethics already fashions and delimits the very question of what we consider to be ethical or potentially ethical in the first place. Circular as it sounds, the approach we take necessarily determines to a large extent what it is we are approaching. While the history of ethical thought has consisted of a vast variety of different perspectives, it could be argued that these can be clustered and thus understood as distinct modes of thinking the ethical.

We might, for instance, focus our thinking of the ethical on behaviour or we might focus it on character. If we follow the former perspective, then what is ethical lies in what we do, how we act. The important question of ethics is, then, *what should I do?* Or *how should I act?* Or perhaps *how should people in general act?* Or *how should we teach or allow people to act?* If, on the other hand, we follow the latter perspective, we would see ethics as concerned with who we are. The salient questions then are something like, *what kind of person should I be? What kind of person is it right to become? What habits should I adopt? What temperament should I encourage in myself?* Or even *how should I look upon the world?* While this approach is often seen in terms of self-determination, the focus need not necessarily be on the self. The questions here could be extended to *how should we teach people to be? What type of character should we encourage in the young or in society in general? What should we as a society or a culture value? How should we be?*

Similarly, and to an extent overlapping with this, we might focus our attention on the outcome of actions or, on the contrary, we might focus on the intentions which led to the action. Where we choose to locate the ethical in this way determines to an enormous extent how we think about what is right and wrong, acceptable or unacceptable. There is also a question here of what we determine to be the effect or outcome of an action. It is not always so straightforward.

Take, for extreme example, the experiments conducted at Nazi concentration camps like Dachau and Auschwitz. The Nazis conducted experiments into hypothermia using human prisoners. The received wisdom with regard to someone suffering from hypothermia had been that it was better to rewarm them slowly. The findings from the Nazi experiments contradicted this, demonstrating that in fact rapid rewarming was more effective and more likely to result in survival. However, in order to conduct their experiments and collect the necessary data, the Nazis subjected prisoners to sub-zero temperatures and experimented with a range of different approaches to rewarming and resuscitation, causing extreme suffering and death. In effect, they tortured the prisoners in order to extract seemingly useful scientific data. The immediate outcome of these experiments would be, for the vast majority of the prisoners, pain and death. For the Nazi doctors it would be the data. Most people would condemn these experiments as utterly unethical. That a consequence of the experiments might be an improved understanding of how hypothermia functions and thus the saving of the lives of hypothermic patients, in no way justifies the actions of the Nazi doctors. Where then are we saying the locus of ethics is here?

A straightforward condemnation of the Nazi experiments on the grounds that the experiments caused unspeakable suffering and ultimately death for those experimented upon may seem sufficient here. Such a position, however, is an endorsement of the perspective that the ethically salient moment in relation to the actions of the Nazi doctors actually lies in the outcome of their actions. This would suggest that if the experiment for some reason didn't cause such grave suffering for some of those subjected to it or, as was the case, some didn't die as a direct result of the experiments, then these cases ought to be judged differently. Imagine there are two doctors, each instructed to carry out the same experiment on two different prisoners. The first prisoner suffers intense pain and dies. The second prisoner does not appear to suffer as severely as the first and does not die. Ought we to conclude that the actions of the second doctor are ethically preferable to the actions of the second, simply because the consequences, through no merit or design of the doctor, are preferable? It is difficult to see in what sense such a distinction could be understood as ethically meaningful.

Let us consider another example; the standard scenario of Fox Broadcasting's popular television series *24*. The Counter Terrorism Unit have apprehended a known terrorist who is privy to details of a planned terrorist attack which it is believed will result in the destruction of a major city and thousands of lives. The CTU torture the terrorist, inflicting sufficient suffering to cause him to divulge his secrets. The consequences here may seem favourable. Does this mean that they are ethically acceptable? Many people would argue that it does. Such an argument presupposes adopting a consequentialist position, perhaps with the addition of a certain moral arithmetic – that it is better for one terrorist to suffer than it is for thousands of apparently innocent citizens to die.

It seems then that it might be ethically acceptable to inflict torture if the ends are in themselves seen as right or good. What, then, if we return to our first example and add in a later end. Yes, the use of concentration camp prisoners in hypothermia experiments is ethically unacceptable but if the scientific insights from these experiments, the discovery of 'rapid active warming', save lives, does this start to affect things? If the scientific insights save more lives than those lost, does this change our ethical perspective? How many more would we want to count as more? And over what sort of time period would we count? Presumably, given long enough, the total count of lives saved is likely to exceed the total number of lives lost. If we refuse this calculus, if we maintain that the experiments are simply wrong, simply unacceptable, then we are simply refusing the core of a consequentialist position. This would suggest, for the sake of consistency, that we might want to revisit the second example. If the torture of concentration camp prisoners is simply wrong, then so too, presumably, is the torture of the terrorist. Even if we refuse this equation, we would have to introduce finer detail to support the non-consequentialist stance. We could argue that torturing the terrorist is justifiable because he is a terrorist and, therefore, not party to the same rights as innocent prisoners. But what we cannot do, while remaining consistent, is justify the torture on the basis of what would follow from it. It may seem then that holding a consistent consequentialist perspective is not so easy. The complexity here is mirrored in the developing and diverse history of approaches to ethics which would, differences notwithstanding, be understood as consequentialist. Some forms of consequentialism focus more on the individual, some more on the wider society. Some more overtly entertain, or even promote, the idea of a rule-based system wherein the matter for consideration would not be limited to the direct or even eventual consequences of a specific action, but rather the consideration would be focused on the general acceptance or prohibition of a certain behaviour or way of acting. This admittance of rules into what appears initially a non-rule-based way of thinking actually dates back to early European consequentialists such as William Paley, an early advocate of the idea that, practically speaking, acts ought to permitted or forbidden generally rather than considered on a one-to-one basis (Paley, 1815).

Perhaps the key issue in considering a consequentialist position, other differences aside, is the question of what it is in an action that ought to determine its ethical value. The form of consequentialism best known in the English-speaking world today is what is known as utilitarianism, an approach initially developed in the eighteenth century by Jeremy Bentham, although there are a number of precursors to Bentham's thought both from within and outwith the English tradition. Alternative originators of utilitarianism notwithstanding, Bentham's formulation remains one of the better known and arguably most influential. The basis of Bentham's ethics is what has been termed the *principle of the greatest happiness* or, more formally, *the principle of utility*. That is to say, according to Bentham, the important matter in determining the ethical status or value of an action is the matter of happiness or utility. This is succinctly expressed in Bentham's early work *A Fragment on Government* where he states that 'the greatest happiness of the greatest number ... is the measure of right or wrong' (1988 [1776]: 1). This principle is the axiomatic starting point for his *Introduction to the Principles of Morals and Legislation*.

Bentham vehemently opposed any notion of a natural moral order, famously arguing in his *Anarchical Fallacies* that the very notion of natural and imprescriptible rights (i.e. rights which would be inherent and irremovable) is 'optimific non-sense on stilts' (Bentham, 1988 [1843]: 5). What does, for Bentham, form a basis of an approach to ethics is the seemingly simple principle of seeking to increase, and avoid the decrease of, happiness. That is to say, in Bentham's own words, the principle of utility is:

> that principle which approves or disapproves of every action whatsoever, according to the tendency which it appears to have to augment or diminish the happiness of the party whose interest is in question ... I say of every action whatsoever; and therefore not only of every action of a private individual, but of every measure of government.
>
> (Bentham, 1996 [1781]: 1)

Three crucial points emerge from this short quotation. First, Bentham is clearly indicating a basic measure of what he sees as the good. The good for Bentham is not some abstract and ephemeral notion but is concretely bedded in experience. Good is 'simply' that which leads to pleasure or happiness. Assuming something of a straightforward continuum here, good could also be understood as that which decreases pain, displeasure or unhappiness. Bentham's ethics is not, however, merely descriptive. This is the second point. It is not only that, were I to act, I ought to choose the course that will produce the most happiness, or the least unhappiness. Bentham's ethics is restless, his argument assuming the force of an imperative; I should act when I can act to produce an increase in happiness, I should refrain from acting when there is no such benefit. In the terms of the theory itself, an action which has no impact on happiness one way or the other is not neutral but lacks utility and is, therefore, wasteful. Third, Bentham is clear to point out the relevant beneficiary of all this happiness. In referring to the party whose interest is in question, Bentham does not mean to say that we need only consider the actor or those who would motivate the action. What he is saying is that in enacting his principle we need to take into account everyone who might be affected. So, we have an expression of a basic value (pleasure is good), a duty (to engage in useful action) and a statement of scope (all those reasonably thought to be affected).

Simple as the notion of maximising pleasure may initially sound, Bentham was aware that pleasure is actually quite complex. To help operationalise his principle then, he laid out what he considered to be the basic relevant axes of pleasure:

1   intensity
2   duration
3   certainty
4   propinquity
5   fecundity
6   purity
7   extent

These axes allow us to distinguish between competing pleasures. The intensity with which we are likely to experience the pleasure clearly affects the value we place on that pleasure. Put simply, it would seem commonsensical to accept that the more intense a pleasure is, the more, for want of a better term, pleasurable it is. We might, however, raise the question of limits. Might it not be the case that after a certain point an intensity of pleasure begins to blur with displeasure? Or, at the very least, that the terminology of pleasure/displeasure and happiness/ unhappiness becomes inadequate to the experience? This idea, or experience, certainly problematises Bentham's argument and allows us to see the limits of his assumptions. There is what we might term a polite veil placed over the understanding of human pleasure here. Such a veil not only points to what may not be included in Bentham's formula but, more troublingly, it cannot but undermine the formula from the inside. Let us, however, remain for the moment with Bentham.

Just as it might seem obvious that a more intense pleasure, all else being equal, is more pleasurable than a less intense pleasure, so too a pleasure which lasts a longer time is probably more pleasurable, all other factors being equal, than a pleasure which lasts a shorter time. Taken together, these first two axes allow a sense of quantity of pleasure. Jumping out of an aeroplane might facilitate a rather intense experience of pleasure compared to sunbathing on a beach. The parachute jump, however, would likely be over quite quickly whereas, with the correct suntan lotion, you could enjoy the beach for hours. Where intensity is equal, choosing between courses of action could be a simple step of considering the time, and when the time is equal, it would be a simple matter of considering the predicted intensity. When the factors vary, however, when you attempt to compare a long pleasurable experience with a short but more intensely pleasurable one, Bentham's proposed calculus seems significantly less practicable.

Certainty seems a similarly obvious and, at least on its own, perhaps more workable criterion to apply. Given the choice between two or more courses of action, it makes some sense to choose the one which is more likely to actually result in pleasure. Choosing between two restaurants, it would make some sense to opt for the one you have enjoyed before. The other may serve exceptional food but, assuming no reliable recommendations, there is something of a gamble involved. Clearly the matter of what is at stake comes in here and thus certainty becomes attached in some way to intensity and/or duration. You may be more inclined to sample an unknown and not extortionate wine than you would be to try an utterly unknown holiday destination.

Perhaps less obviously, Bentham also advocated prioritising those pleasures which are temporally closer. The pleasure I can experience today, all else being equal, trumps the pleasure I could experience tomorrow. We need to keep in mind, though, the potential for increased pleasure further down the line. Eating your chicken today might satisfy the rule of propinquity but maintaining your chicken and enjoying eggs for years to come might make more sense.

Being realistic, we also do need to consider the fact that real life experience is not always as cut and dried as abstract examples. Something may well bring with it a certain quota of pleasure, but it also might entail a certain amount of displeasure. As much as I enjoy fresh fish, I find the experience of descaling irritating and the experience of gutting unpleasant. In Bentham's system this would be a rather impure pleasure, mixing as it does pleasure with displeasure. Were I to have someone else prepare my fish for me, this might alleviate the displeasurable dimension and render the experience as a whole purer and, thus, more pleasurable.

Finally, as suggested in the above clarification of Bentham's reference to 'the party whose interest is in question', it is important to discern who and how many are to be affected by the action and, crucially, how they are affected. Are they affected positively or negatively? Is this effect intense or moderate? Is it brief or does it persist over some time? Does it come sooner or later? How likely is it that the effect on those immediately touched will produce in turn further pleasures, either for them or for others? And to what extent is the pleasure derived from the activity essentially mixed with displeasure.

Importantly, Bentham was reluctant to make any inherent distinction between pleasures, such as high or low pleasures. As overtly subjective as it is overtly egalitarian, his view was that the pleasure felt was the pleasure which counted, not any external value imputed to that pleasure or the object or activity from which it is derived. Taken purely at a specular level, there is no difference between watching a football match and, say, watching Tarkovsky's *Stalker*. Insofar as the ones watching them each derive the same degree of pleasure from the experience, there is no real difference, except for the fact that Tarkovsky's film is rather longer than a normal football match, so is presumably preferable for the utilitarian.

One common objection to Bentham's argument is that this insistence on the equality of pleasures is counterintuitive or, at least, runs counter to our common way of seeing the world and, by extension, how we make decisions in it. If all pleasures are of equal value, then not only is there no way to distinguish between different classes of activity but, moreover, there is no way to distinguish between different classes of affected parties. On the kind of cursory reading I have given above, it might seem that Bentham is making the perfectly acceptable point that all people are equal and ought to be treated equally. His argument, however, logically extends far beyond this. If all pleasures are equal, then, logically, it doesn't matter who or what is experiencing the pleasure. This would suggest then that animals count just as much in Bentham's calculus as people. As counterintuitive as this may seem to many today, we should perhaps keep in mind that Bentham was writing at a time when slavery had not yet been outlawed in his country. Bentham himself makes this point rather neatly. Sidestepping questions of the killing of animals for food or safety, he argues that there is no justification for inflicting suffering on animals. Drawing a comparison with slaves, he suggests that the same change in perspective which brings us to acknowledge that there is no supportable argument for slavery, might also bring us to recognise that there is no supportable argument for inflicting suffering on animals. It might be argued that, unlike slaves or people who look different, animals do differ from *us* in that they lack the faculties of reason and discourse. This, however, Bentham contends, is irrelevant. What is relevant, in a utilitarian view, is the pleasure/pain axis. Animals suffer. That's what counts, not what they could reason or say in the face of such suffering. Bentham's point here perhaps takes on a clearer hue if we consider human infants who equally can neither speak nor reason but whose suffering we would be more commonly inclined to protect against.

Of course one could always argue that human activities will tend to be more future oriented and productive than animal activities and, therefore, that (certain) human pleasures are more likely to lead to the increase and broader spread of pleasures. Similarly, on the flip side, human suffering is likely to lead to a broader spread of greater suffering. Bentham would agree. This is precisely what he intends with his fifth criterion, fecundity. What this points to, however, is an extrinsic valuation. That a human pleasure may appear more valued because it is more fecund suggests precisely that it is not actually more valuable in itself but is only more valuable insofar as its effects are more abundant. Studying psychology, for example, may seem more worthy than working on a supermarket checkout but, for Bentham, it is only so because it or, rather, *if* it has the effect of producing more benefit, more pleasure, than the alternative. An academic pursuit is not intrinsically better or more valuable, it is only so in certain conditions.

While there is a cleanness or straightforwardness to Bentham's endeavour to formulate an ethics, some might argue that it is simply unrealistic. It may be philosophically convenient to reduce all pleasures to the same level but, arguably, this is not how we live. Bentham's successor in utilitarianism, John Stuart Mill, was of this opinion and sought to develop utilitarian thinking in such a way as to address this issue. Animal and human pleasures, Mill argued, are not equivalent. Bentham famously kept a pig as a pet. As fond as he may have been of his pig, it seems unlikely that he would have happily traded places with it. As happy as the pig appears rolling in the mud, it seems unlikely that the philosopher would easily renounce his studies to join him. And yet, doesn't Bentham's own argument suggest that he would? One could imagine that Bentham might at this point invoke the rule of fecundity. Mill, on the other hand, insists that the relevant point is intrinsic, not extrinsic; '[f]ew human creatures would consent to be changed into any of the lower animals, for a promise of the fullest allowance of a beast's pleasure' (Mill, 1861: 139). This distinction of higher and lower applies not only to interspecific comparisons. Mill is keen to separate pleasures themselves into higher and lower orders. The obvious point Mill seems to miss here is that of relevance or appropriacy. Were Bentham magically turned into a pig, presumably he would be perfectly happy rolling in the mud, as he would be a pig and thus content with piggish pleasures.

For Mill, however, there is a more intrinsic distinction to be made. Intelligence and refinement, what Mill refers to as the higher faculties, grant access to pleasures which are superior in quality. Mill argues here that part of the confusion in Bentham's position is the oversimplification caused by using the term 'happiness' too broadly. We need, he argues, to distinguish between happiness and contentment (Mill, 1861: 140). Those, people or animals, of lower faculties may well have their satisfactions met more easily than people of higher faculties but this is precisely because they are of a different order. An educated and refined person, unhappy as they may be with their lot, could not be satisfied with the same pleasures as would satisfy a less educated or refined person. While it would be perfectly possible to flip this point and argue that the less refined and educated person may equally be attached to their particular pleasures, Mill refuses this on the grounds that the less educated and refined person cannot appreciate the pleasures of the educated and refined person whereas the educated and refined person would choose from an informed position and dignity would disincline a person from reversing down this qualitative slope. For Mill, then, it simply is better to be a dissatisfied philosopher than a satisfied fool.

Curiously, as convincing as Mill's argument sounds in the abstract, populating it with contemporary examples makes it sound unacceptably unPC. Better a dissatisfied psychology professor than a satisfied burger chef? The question of political correctness unravels in various directions here. We might quietly agree with this point – how many would honestly prefer for their child a career in fast food over a career in higher education? – while more vocally pointing to the real social conditions masked in posing the question as so straightforward in the first place – how many really make a conscious choice between two such distinct careers? Moreover, the apparently intuitive gravitation toward the choice of psychology professor sidesteps or assumes all too quickly an answer to the question of fecundity. Is it really so unproblematically the case that the work of the psychology professor sows the seeds for a greater happiness for a wider population? Much that is erroneous, misleading and downright harmful might be understood to have emerged from psychology. Promulgating and extending this knowledge ought, perhaps, not to go unquestioned. Which is not, of course, to ignore the many malign issues with the fast-food industry. The two are, perhaps, on some levels not so dissimilar, willing parties in an individualising, consumer-based system which prioritises superficial efficiency and speed of delivery over long-term benefits.

Returning to Mill, however, his point, essentially, is that intelligence provides access to a higher order of pleasure and the appreciation of that pleasure. While many people appear to be perfectly happy (or content) watching competitive reality television shows, considerably fewer people appear to be perfectly happy watching Béla Tarr films. Not only do fewer people watch them, but there is less whooping and cheering evident in the arthouse cinemas and, as intellectually stimulated and impressed as one might feel watching *Sátántangó*, I doubt many people leave the screening with ear-to-ear grins. But Mill is arguing that the fans of *X Factor* experience a lesser pleasure. The arthouse cinema-goer may not seem as happy but they are just less content. They are actually more happy because the pleasure they are experiencing is of a greater type. We know this because the person choosing to watch the Béla Tarr film would not choose to watch *X Factor* instead. The person choosing to watch *X Factor*, we might imagine, would similarly not choose to watch *Sátántangó*. The difference, however, lies in their ability to make an informed choice. Pretty much anyone can grasp the satisfactions offered by reality TV. Not everyone can grasp the satisfactions offered by complex metaphorical ruminations on Hungarian communism and human desire. Moreover, and this is Mill's crucial point, only the Tarr viewer can grasp the qualitative distinction between the two and appreciate the superiority of their own preference. The *X Factor* viewer's disagreement here would be dismissed as being down to a lack of appreciation of a higher pleasure they were simply ill-equipped to appreciate.

What these contemporary examples perhaps allows us to appreciate is the assumption of value already supposed in the examples. The pleasures of a higher-order creature are necessarily higher-order pleasures and the proof of this is that the higher-order creature would not choose to demean themselves by relinquishing their access to these pleasures in favour of lower-order pleasures. Not only is the argument necessarily presented from the 'higher-order' perspective and therefore pre-inclined towards that with which it assumes an identity (i.e. the higher-order creatures) but, in addition, there appears to be a certain circularity to Mill's logic. Higher-order creatures are those who are endowed, whether by nature or learning, with a greater intellectual capability. Higher-order pleasures are those pleasures which would be preferred by a higher-order creature. Higher-order pleasures are greater in value than lower-order pleasures. We know this because higher-order creatures value them so.

When the higher-order creature under consideration here is a human being in relation to a lower-order creature such as a pig, this doesn't seem so contentious. When the higher-order creature is a human being placed in comparative relation to another less educated or less intelligent human being, then suddenly it seems somewhat more problematic. If, as the utilitarians from Bentham through to Mill and beyond contest, what counts is the maximising of pleasure, then, in Mill's argument, not only are refined or intellectual pleasures more intrinsically valuable and thus count for more but, consequently, the recipient of those pleasures is valued higher or, at least, set to benefit more often and more intensely. This seems to suggest then that the higher-order creature is not only more refined and more intelligent but is also more valued and thus more valuable. They are more valued, however, based on a calculus which would posit them as the primary evaluators.

So, while Mill's reworking of Bentham's ethics, with its clarification of the greatest happiness principle, cunningly sidesteps the supposedly problematic levelling of human and animal statuses, it cannot but also reintroduce the rather problematic hierarchisation between people and potentially run the risk of validating the very kinds of racism to which Bentham was timeously opposed. Lest we forget, the assumption of base and natural differences between populations is not something safely consigned to the past. As recently as 1971 the esteemed professor of psychology Hans Eysenck confidently described the idea of racial equality as 'a myth', with 'no scientific evidence to support it' (Eysenck, 1971: 20).

Already, in Bentham's approach, there is a curious problem concerning what we might call the collision of pleasures. Let us say, for example, that I derive an enormous amount of pleasure from inflicting minor pain on someone. Following the basic calculus of Bentham's utilitarianism, my actions would be warranted. It is certainly not difficult to square such a scenario with Bentham's seven axes. This would appear to give a certain licence to non-consensual sadism as long as the sadist in question was careful always to ensure that the suffering they inflicted never outweighed the pleasure they derived from inflicting it. In Mill's version of utilitarianism, this problem can be understood to be exacerbated. While Mill would no doubt count the joys of sadism as a rather base pleasure and thus circumvent the problems of this particular scenario, the problem continues in other applications. Imagine, for example, that a team of researchers wished to explore the effects of low-level pain on concentration. The result of this experiment could be understood not only to be rather beneficial in its potential applications but, in addition, the experiment and the plaudits it would bring to the researchers could be understood to be quite immediately pleasurable. Assuming that kudos, career benefits and the simple satisfaction of accomplishing research result in a significant quantity of pleasure, we could understand that the scales clearly tip in favour of the experimenters and, therefore, that it is quite legitimate for them to inflict pain, as long as it is not too much pain, and that they would not necessarily require any consent in order to do so.

Mill introduces a second major principle which might be understood in some ways to moderate this kind of problem. He calls this second principle the harm principle. He states this as follows:

> the sole end for which mankind are warranted, individually or collectively, in interfering with the liberty of action of any of their number, is self-protection. That the only purpose for which power can be rightfully exercised over any member of a civilised community, against his will, is to prevent harm to others. His own good, either physical or moral, is not a sufficient warrant. He cannot rightfully be compelled to do or forbear because it will be better for him to do so, because it will make him happier, because, in the opinion of others, to do so would be wise, or even right.
>
> (Mill, 1859: 14)

Where the principle of the greatest happiness would seek to maximise social happiness and, in itself, could be understood to give licence to the exploitation of minorities or individuals as long as such exploitation was in the service of a greater total pleasure, the harm principle sets a clear limit on this. While it has been argued that Mill's two arguments actually work against each other (Warburton, 2014; 162), this is not necessarily the case. Following Bentham, Mill is concerned with the maximisation of happiness, of pleasure in the widest possible scope. This means that his focus is on humanity en masse, not on the plight of the individual. The harm principle, presented in isolation, appears to be concerned less with the promotion of the benefits of the whole and more with the protection of the individual. It should, however, be understood in context. Mill's real concern is that we ought to be unshackled from social constraints, that we ought to be free to do as we wish, to pursue our interests and whims as we see fit. This *freedom to* requires a *freedom from* the restraints of the society in which we find ourselves. Not only is such a *freedom to* immediately beneficial to each individual, insofar as we assume that, at least within our power or ability, we would pursue our own pleasures, but, moreover, the *freedom to* is also essential, in Mill's view, to the progress of humanity; 'utility in its largest sense [is] grounded on the permanent interests of man as a progressive being' (Mill, 1859: 15). That is, it is in the interests of all humanity to make progress in matters of technology, politics and even morals (these are Mill's own examples) and this progress is best supported by ensuring the liberty of the individual or particular collectives. This is Mill's main emphasis: we should be free to pursue our pleasures and those things which may well enhance the pleasures of the masses in time. The harm principle is introduced as a limitation on this freedom. Effectively Mill's point is that unbounded freedom would lead to a widespread reduction in pleasure. Not only would those directly harmed by others' pursuits suffer but the persistent generalised threat which would be felt by all, would necessarily lead to an overall reduction in pleasure. So, a safeguard is required.

This is important in relation to human research ethics as it is often perceived to be the key principle governing research involving human participants, such as psychological research. Without ever citing him explicitly, the British Psychological Society (BPS) and American Psychological Association (APA) both make clear reference to the principle Mill is expounding. The fourth principle of the BPS's code of ethics relating specifically to human research is 'Maximising benefit and minimising harm' (BPS, 2010: 11). The first principle of the APA code is 'Beneficence and Nonmaleficence' (APA, 2010: 3). The BPS expands on the basic statement of its principle to boldly assert that 'Harm to research participants must be avoided' (BPS, 2010: 11). This is immediately adjusted with the suggestion that, at times, the risk of harm may be an unavoidable element in some research and the acknowledgement that, at times, there may be tensions between 'the legitimate needs of research and the avoidance of risk' (BPS, 2010: 11). Ultimately, the authors of the code suggest, in a direct invocation of Mill, that 'researchers will need to consider the costs to the individual participant versus potential societal benefits' (BPS, 2010: 12). The APA, similarly, acknowledge the possibility of conflicts amongst the psychologist's concerns and advocate that, in such circumstances, they resolve such conflicts in a manner which at least minimises harm (APA, 2010: 3).

Understanding the secondary nature of Mill's limiting clause seems essential to understanding the force of this key principle. It appears that safeguarding the wellbeing of participants is, like Mill's harm principle, something which ultimately has to be formulated within a context. Where for Mill the context is the potential for human or social progress, for the BPS and APA the context is the pursuit of their own interests, i.e. psychology. Moreover, where for Mill the harm principle, however much it is logically secondary to the principle of utility, is absolute, this is not how the discipline of psychology appears to treat it. The only limitation Mill admits for the harm principle is the harm principle itself. That is to say, I have no right to interfere with or to cause any harm to another except insofar as to protect myself from their interference or their infliction of harm upon me. Psychology, on the other hand, appears to posit its own pursuit of its own knowledge construction and fortification as legitimate grounds upon which to risk harming those participating in its research. In keeping with its utilitarian basis, the BPS suggests that, ultimately, when there is a tension between the demands of the research and the potential of harm to participants, the researchers resort to a utilitarian cost–benefit calculus.

The consideration of utilitarianism laid out so far is, however, rather incomplete. It has only focused on the questions of determination and authorisation, not on the question of obligation. That is, we have primarily considered the question of how we can determine the best course of action. The utilitarian answer is, of course, that we must perform a moral calculation that would determine from which action the greatest good would result. We have also considered the question of harm and the limits utilitarianism, at least in Mill's version of it, places on otherwise utilitarian action. That is, we have considered the question of what action I am authorised or have the right to take. What we have not considered is the question of duty, the question of what action I am perhaps obliged to take.

If, however, we wish to pursue a utilitarian line, then this not a question we can avoid. Utilitarianism, from Bentham through to Mill and beyond, presents an overarching theory of what is right. In its simplest form, as we have seen, this is can be expressed as maximising the greatest happiness for the greatest number. This is not, however, simply what we ought to do when we decide to act and encounter some dilemma. It is, for the utilitarian, what we ought to do, per se, all of the time. Take the somewhat clichéd example of the burning building with trapped occupants. Imagine there is an old man and a young boy in the building. Utilitarianism does not simply provide us with a tool to calculate which of the two it would be best to help were we to feel courageous enough to intervene at all. It tells us that, if the consequence of our action is likely to promote greater happiness or wellbeing, then it is imperative that we help.

This obligatory dimension of utilitarianism might be seen to make it quite demanding and certainly makes it a more forceful theory than it is usually taken to be. The BPS Code of Human Research Ethics appears to stand behind this arduous notion of duty in its assertion that 'Psychological knowledge must be generated and used for beneficial purposes' (BPS, 2010: 10). At least, it does if the 'must' here is understood in the strong sense. One wonders, however, to what extent this compelling dimension of utilitarian thought actually impinges on psychological practice in practice. How often are research projects initiated primarily from a motivation to benefit? How often are research projects closed down when they are no longer convincingly benefiting anyone? Certainly academic advancement is aided by landing large grants and well-placed publications, raising at least the temptation to factor in one's own, over the greater, happiness. That there is a widely reported tendency to favour the dissemination of 'positive' results would seem to support the suspicion that the duty to pursue the greatest good is not actually something which weighs terribly heavily in the reality of the world of research, psychological or otherwise.

This application of utilitarian thought notwithstanding, there is a much more fundamental problem with utilitarianism and consequentialism more broadly. Long before Mill's refashioning of Bentham's theory and even before Bentham's own work, David Hume postulated that it is not possible to derive an *ought* from an *is*. Applied to utilitarian theory we could understand this as reminding us that the fact that something is desired does not in any way tell us that it is ethically correct to desire it. G.E. Moore (1903) makes this point with explicit reference to Mill in his famous discussion of the naturalistic fallacy. Mill, as we have seen, attempts to derive a notion of the good from what is desirable or what produces happiness. Given that happiness is, in Mill's argument, the only thing that can be desired in itself, these are ultimately the same. Effectively, then, Mill is saying that we know the good because we know what is desirable and what is desirable at the end of the day always comes down to happiness. Moore objects to this equation of good and desirable.

> Well, the fallacy in this step is so obvious, that it is quite wonderful how Mill failed to see it. The fact is that 'desirable' does not mean 'able to be desired' as 'visible' means 'able to be seen'. The desirable means simply what *ought* to be desired or *deserves* to be desired; just as the detestable means not what can be but what ought to be detested and the damnable what deserves to

be damned. Mill has, then, smuggled in, under cover of the word 'desirable', the very notion about which he ought to be quite clear. 'Desirable' does indeed mean 'what it is good to desire'; but when this is understood, it is no longer plausible to say that our only test of *that*, is what is actually desired. Is it merely a tautology when the Prayer Book talks of *good* desires? Are not *bad* desires also possible? Nay, we find Mill himself talking of a 'better and nobler object of desire', as if, after all, what is desired were not *ipso facto* good, and good in proportion to the amount it is desired. Moreover, if the desired is *ipso facto* the good; then the good is *ipso facto* the motive of our actions, and there can be no question of finding motives for doing it, as Mill is at such pains to do. If Mill's explanation of 'desirable' be *true*, then his statement that the rule of action may be *confounded* with the motive of it is untrue; for the motive of action will then be according to him *ipso facto* its rule; there can be no distinction between the two, and therefore no confusion, and thus he has contradicted himself flatly. These are specimens of the contradictions, which, as I have tried to shew, must always follow from the use of the naturalistic fallacy; and I hope I need now say no more about the matter.

(Moore, 1903: 67)

Moore's point is straightforward enough. It takes little imagination to conjure up an example of something which is desired by someone but which is not necessarily thought to be good. Mill himself seems to already acknowledge this point when he introduces the notion of higher- and lower-order pleasures. If what is desired were simply good because it is desired then there would be no possibility of distinguishing qualitatively between pleasures or desires; they would simply, as in Bentham, be good because they were desired. If we take desirable to mean that which it is good to desire, rather than simply what is desired, then we cannot conclude that the desirable is good without merely repeating what we have already assumed. Furthermore, if the good is defined as what is desired then there is scarcely a need for a theory of ethics or really for any consideration of ethics at all. If what is desired is, by dint of the fact that it is desired, good, assuming people tend to act in accordance with their interests or desires, then what people do would inevitably be good. Ethics, for the utilitarian at least, would then be nothing but the calculation of which good to promote above other competing goods. The problem here is that the additional step of prioritising exceeds the initial determination or assumption of what is good. If the good is reducible to what is desirable, that is, then all goods, just as all desires, are equal. My good doesn't become less good simply because there are more of you than me, unless we choose to smuggle in a further assumption that a greater number of desirers results in a greater intensity of goodness.

Utilitarianism, by this account, appears to be somewhat circular. If we add to this problematic equation of desire and good the fact that consequentialist ethics can be used to sanction all kinds of undesirable behaviours, as long as these behaviours result in desirable outcomes, then utilitarianism appears to be thoroughly ethically bankrupt from the off. We might even say that what is presented as a theory of ethics is effectively a theory without ethics. Of course, we could argue that, problematic as it seems, the utilitarian perspective is actually a necessary bottom line and the only real possibility once we have dispensed with mystic notions of an absolute or divinely determined good. If the good is not somehow out there, already formed and ready to be known, then perhaps it makes sense to say that there is no good as such. We may still, however, want to manage our society and utilitarianism, although seemingly somewhat squeamish about formulating its own potential in this nihilistic manner, is actually adequate to this task. This, however, is to posit utilitarianism as a juridical theory rather than a theory of ethics. The calculations and choices delivered by utilitarian processes necessarily remain external to the actor. This fact results in two crucial points; the responsibility for the calculation resides with the process or system, not with the party involved, and the system itself cannot account for the choice to act. Although from the beginning Bentham is keen to declare utilitarianism's imperative status, in matters of the law there is always the rule to be obeyed and, necessarily distinct from this, the choice whether or not to obey the rule.

This is perhaps, however, to assume too quickly that Moore is correct. In attacking Mill's apparent elision of the gap between the desired and the desirable, Moore claims to have exposed Mill's sleight of hand in creating an *ought* from an *is*. Is not Moore himself, however, the one who is guilty of a sleight of hand. Moore wants to argue that we cannot discover the good from examining what is desirable because the very concept of desirable already presupposes an idea of the good. He predicates this line of argument on the fact that the term 'desirable' does not mean, as he supposes Mill to suppose, that which can be desired but rather that which ought to be desired or that which it is good to desire. Understood in this way, the offending tautology is clear. Is Moore right, though? In order to be desirable in Moore's definition of the term, the thing in question would have to be capable of being desired. The distinction, then, is the extent to which you accept differences in perspectives in relation to questions of desire. On this reading, Moore appears to be assuming a universal or, at least, social consensus. If Moore is understood to be saying that there are simply things which are good to desire, this would be to say that the good exists outside of our determination of it. That is, it would be to return us to a religious conception of ethics or, perhaps better, morality. If, however, he is understood to be advocating consensus and arguing that the socially determined idea of what is desirable is what ought to hold sway, then he has not really moved very far from Mill. The fundamental mechanism of utilitarianism is, after all, the process of the calculation of social utility.

This, again, would seem to place utilitarianism on the side of law, rather than ethics. The narrow gap which persists, however, can be located in the desire to implement or adhere to the utilitarian system itself. It is not so much a question of whether or not desire can be equated with or reduced to the good. Rather it is a problem of how to account for the desire to accept or reject the calculus. This dilemma can already be discerned in Mill's introduction of a hierarchy of pleasures. Mill's own desire refuses the level playing field advocated by Bentham. Clearly, this desire cannot be accounted for within the system itself.

What this then brings to light is that persisting under the clear logic of juridical utilitarianism is an excluded and incalculable moment, a moment which must present for each individual or entity who would entertain a utilitarian move. If, with Mill, we agree that good is what brings happiness, and desire is always, ultimately, desire for happiness, then ethics would appear to reduce to the question of the extent to which one has acted in accordance with one's desire. This is where utilitarianism meets ethics. If your desire to endorse the utilitarian perspective trumps or exceeds your other desires, then you might reasonably ask, what is it you truly desire?

6

THE GOOD WILL

If ethics *qua* ethics cannot be determined through appeal to what is, then either it cannot be determined at all or it must be determined in a manner independent of any experience. Exploring the possibility of such an *a priori* approach to ethics was precisely the project of Immanuel Kant.

Steering away from the idea of trying to ground an ethics in what is, Kant necessarily steers away from a focus on action and concerns himself with what drives or wills that action. This is to say, Kant's perspective is very much not a consequentialist ethics. At the simplest level, there is always potentially an aleatory dimension to optimific acts and this renders consequence a rather peculiar measure of the ethical. For Kant, the focus of the ethical (or moral, as he terms it) needs to be on the will to act (or to refrain from acting), not on the act itself. And for a will to be truly ethical, that will has to be good in itself.

This is to say, among other things, that what determines the good as good must transcend or sit outside of actual experience or human nature. Keen to avoid any insupportable mystic solution here, such as appeals to God or gods, Kant argues that the good is purely rational. Being purely rational means that the good must be the good for all rational creatures. It is not contingent on any particular circumstance or nature; not the circumstance of our age, or our planet, not even the nature of being human. A rational ethics would hold true for any rational species anywhere, at any time. Kant terms this pure rationality the Moral Law. The ethical is, then, that which is in absolute accord with the Moral Law. Moreover, Kant argues, it is necessary to be in accord with the Moral Law through choice and for that choice to be the sole motivator behind one's actions.

Imagine you jump into a fast-flowing river to save a drowning child, to use one of our examples from earlier. This would probably seem to most people a good thing to do. For Kant, however, it is only a good thing to do if you jumped into the river to save the drowning child because you knew it was your moral duty to do so. If you jumped into the river to save the child because you thought it might make you look good, would impress your friends and get you on television or even because you cared for the child, then, from a Kantian perspective, it is no longer a moral act. To further distinguish this perspective from the utilitarians, we should also keep in mind that for Kant it is not essential that you actually save the drowning child. What counts is the will or intention to save them. Where the consequentialist, obviously, would be primarily focused on the outcome, Kant is concerned with choice and motivation. This is famously illustrated, and clarified, in Kant's discussion of lying in *On A Supposed Right to Lie Because of Philanthropic Concerns*.

Kant argues that telling the truth is a universal duty. Now, of course, it is quite obvious that in some scenarios telling the truth might well result in a less desirable consequence. To stick with the example made famous by Kant himself, imagine a murderer is pursuing your friend. Your friend comes and hides out in your house. When the murderer comes knocking at your door, asking for your friend's whereabouts, what do you do? What we might imagine as the common response here, and certainly that advocated by Kant's interlocutor, Constant, would be to lie to the murderer. Not only would this appear the correct reaction for the simple reason that we would presumably want to protect our friend but, so argues Constant, it is also the morally defensible reaction, insofar as there can be no right to provide what would ultimately be harm-inducing information. If we know that the murderer's intention is to kill or even harm our friend, then we cannot be bound by any duty of truth-telling, precisely because of this probable consequence. It is here that Kant flatly disagrees. For Kant, our duty is to tell the truth. That the caller intends to use the information to apprehend and kill our friend ought not to affect this. We cannot know in advance the consequence of our choices but we can determine whether or not we make these choices in accordance with the Moral Law.

Imagine you determine to lie to the murderer with the intention of, through your lie, sending him in the wrong direction and thus protecting your friend. You tell the murderer that your friend is not in your house. The murder, believing you, goes to look for your friend elsewhere. Unfortunately, unbeknownst to you, your friend has already snuck out of the house to make his escape. Following your misdirection, the murder now meets and kills your friend. The consequence of your lie here is precisely that which you sought to avoid.

Clearly, had you told the truth in the above scenario, it would have been to your friend's advantage. This, however, is not the point. The point is rather that we cannot predetermine the outcome, and by intervening with a lie, we cannot but assume culpability for what follows. Imagine the alternative scenario with the equally undesirable consequence, wherein we tell the murderer the truth of (our knowledge of) our friend's whereabouts and our friend is still in the house as we believed. Here we have led the murder straight to our friend but done so in accordance with our perceived duty to tell the truth. While the consequence in the two scenarios is the same, this, for Kant, does not render them at all equal. Neither is it the intention which can, on an ethical level, allow us to distinguish the scenarios. It is simply the adherence to duty.

Consequence is not exactly irrelevant here. But its relevance, or perhaps better said, its significance, is determined by our adherence or lack of adherence to the Moral Law. If I adhere to the Moral Law and tell the truth then the consequence does not, for Kant, issue from this choice. In order to consider the choice presented here from an ethical perspective at all, it must offer itself up to a clearly determinable consideration. The actual consequences of any engagement must remain unpredeterminable. The intention or desired concrete outcome, uncoupled from any actual consequence, is moot. All we can really consider is the abstract moral duty. If following this abstract duty leads to an undesired or undesirable consequence, this is clearly unfortunate but the ultimate, logical consequence of endorsing the potential right to lie is much graver. Put simply, the argument in defence of lying renders all communication, truthful or not, debilitatingly suspect. If lying is justified, then all speech has to be treated as (potentially) deceitful and if all speech is treated as potentially deceitful, then my attempt to misdirect the murderer is always already caught up in an imaginary game of double bluff and topples immediately into nonsense. It is only the assumption of the truth of speech which renders the deceit, however indefensible, possible.

Translating this strict emphasis on moral duty into the field of research, we can begin to understand that Kant's ethics is rather hard to implement in any institutional fashion. In principle it seems straightforward enough to see that what Kant would advocate is a research programme which is driven by the Moral Law and is not motivated by any other factors such as kudos, career or even intrinsic curiosity. In practice, however, it seems impossible that we could ever know what really drove the choices to engage in the research and to design it this way rather than that way. That is, how would anyone but the actor know what motivation lay behind the work?

While in terms of implementing an institutional code of ethics, one with external checks in place, Kant's approach to ethics is clearly unworkable, this is not a concern for Kant. It also doesn't necessarily render Kant's ethics entirely inapplicable to institutional codes. You cannot know, and therefore cannot ensure, that someone is acting purely out of duty towards the Moral Law, but you can still use the more concrete principles Kant derives from his rational approach to map out some contours of an ethical code. This is very much what a number of governing bodies in the field of psychology and beyond seem to have, more or less explicitly, if rather selectively, done.

In his *Grounding for the Metaphysics of Morality,* Kant presents a number of unfolding principles or what he terms categorical imperatives. The first and most general of these is formulated as follows:

> Act only according to that maxim whereby you can at the same time will that it should become a universal law.
>
> (Kant, 1993 [1785]: 30)

The imperative is categorical in the sense that it is not predicated on any conditions. A conditional or hypothetical imperative would necessarily be limited to the particularities of the circumstances. If you want to pass your exams, you should work hard. If you want to lose weight, you should eat less simple carbohydrates. If you want to get into heaven, you should do more good deeds. None of these describes an absolute but only a means to an end. Kant's imperative ought to be followed for no reason other than the fact that it is our duty to do so. The imperative itself is really nothing other than the stipulation of pure rationality which Kant argues must underpin any viable morality. The implication in the statement, and the way the imperative is sometimes translated, is that the maxim could become a universal law without contradiction. If it were to allow of contradiction, then, logically, it would not actually be universal. This stipulation of non-contradiction in relation to the universalisation of the maxim entails two important dimensions. Kant refers to these as contradictions in conception and contradictions in will.

Some actions are so constituted that their maxims cannot without contradiction even be thought as a universal law of nature, much less be willed as what should become one. In the case of others this internal impossibility is indeed not found, but there is still no possibility of willing that their maxim be raised to the universality of a law of nature, because such a will would contradict itself.

(Kant, 1993 [1785]: 32)

A contradiction in conception then is one where the maxim could not be acted upon were it to be universalised. That is to say, the very thing I am seeking to will is logically blocked through the universalising process. A straightforward instance of such a contradiction would be the notion of monopoly. Clearly I cannot will that everyone has the moral right to the monopoly of a particular resource as the monopoly, by definition, can only be held by one party. In a simple domestic setting, my intention of eating all the chocolate cannot be reconciled with the categorical imperative because if I eat all the chocolate, then there is no logical possibility of you eating all the chocolate. The contradiction lies in the very conception of that which I would seek to universalise.

A more complex but highly significant example of a contradiction of conception is the aforementioned one of lying. If I wished to tell a lie and thus willed, as a universal maxim, that lying is permissible for all, then the result would not be my successfully deceiving someone so much as the upending of all sensible language use. A lie is only a lie and can only function as such on the basis of the assumption that the norm is to tell the truth. If I will universal lying, then I cancel the possibility of this norm and, logically, with it, the possibility of lying itself. Put simply, if it were perfectly acceptable for everyone to lie all the time, then it would not be rational to believe anything that was said. The notion of a lie in such a world becomes somewhat meaningless.

A contradiction in will, on the other hand, is one where the universalisation of the intention is something no rational being would choose. I may wish to avoid paying tax and could certainly envisage a world where nobody pays tax without this losing any sense but it could be argued that I wouldn't rationally want to live in a world where there was no social infrastructure. The point here is not simply that I would end up with a situation which was unattractive to me. The point is rather that the initial maxim seeks to maximise benefit (to oneself) and its universalisation would, logically, have quite the opposite effect. This is the contradiction.

One of the most commonplace criticisms levelled against the categorical imperative is that it is always possible to formulate your maxim in such a way as to make it rather specific or, at least, to limit its scope. I cannot will the maxim that everyone should be free to steal their breakfast without unleashing chaos but I could perhaps will the maxim that everyone called Calum is free to steal their breakfast without unleashing too much mayhem. Does this mean then that this formulation passes the test? Here we need to remember Kant's focus on will. What is important first and foremost is the motivation to act, not the formula constructed to facilitate or justify the act. In fashioning a very precise formulation to allow my action, I am in no way affecting the will behind the action. I am simply being disingenuous and perhaps even delusionary.

Importantly, Kant's first formulation only really covers the notion of right and thus is intended only as a means to determine whether or not an action is permissible, not whether the action is worthy. For example, I could quite easily will that all healthy people should eat breakfast. While this works as a test of whether my eating breakfast is a morally acceptable thing to do, it hardly elevates a morning meal to the status of a moral duty. If, however, I wished to steal the bread for my breakfast, it is clear that this cannot pass the test of the imperative and, therefore, is not permissible. To will that everyone can steal their breakfast would be to unleash chaos and an unworkable situation and would therefore constitute a contradiction in will. So, the categorical imperative tells me what I have the right to do but it doesn't tell me what it is good to do. Does this then suggest that the categorical imperative is, from a moral perspective, a take-it-or-leave-it tool? Sure, it would be irrational not to follow the imperative, but technically, I can have no duty to behave rationally. This, in a sense then, is Kant's limit. The theory of ethics he unfurls assumes, and is applicable only to, rational beings. To act ethically is to act rationally. To act rationally is, ultimately, to act ethically.

This duty to abide by the categorical imperative, as we have seen, is not derived from any external or experiential appeal. It is really nothing more than a rational or logical conclusion. In Kantian terms, the categorical imperative is purely analytical. At this level, being a purely analytic and *a priori* rational deduction, there can be no content to the categorical imperative. It is a rational means by which to determine the morality of one's intentions. That is all. It doesn't and cannot tell you what to do. The fact that there are, however, two different types of contradiction arising from the categorical imperative, two different ways in which a maxim can fail the test, points towards two different forms of duty. Kant terms these perfect and imperfect duties. A maxim which fails the categorical imperative through a contradiction of conception points towards a perfect duty. A maxim which fails the categorical imperative through a contradiction of will points towards an imperfect duty. Remaining with our examples above, as lying can be understood to constitute a contradiction of conception, then we have a perfect duty not to lie. This means that lying is, always, under all circumstances, impermissible. The attempt to universalise the maxim of lying inevitably leads to a contradiction and, therefore, is irrational. Universalising the maxim to not pay taxes, on the other hand, doesn't necessarily lead to a contradiction. A state wherein taxes aren't paid is quite conceivable, but it delivers an effect which works against the presumed motive. While there might be a benefit (to me) in not paying my taxes, there is (arguably) no such benefit (to me) in no one paying their taxes. Such a contradiction in will then doesn't give rise to a perfect duty, it gives rise to an imperfect duty. It is clear then that a perfect duty is commensurate with remaining rational in the sense that the very maxim willed would consist in an irrational formulation. Contravening such a duty, would be to will the irrational. A contradiction in will, on the other hand, doesn't lead to an impossible, only an irrational, situation. That is, it is perfectly possible to formulate the maxim in a non-contradictory way. It is just that the effect of this would negate the achievement of the very end initially aimed towards. It is still a contradiction and it is still indicative of the irrational. It is, however, for Kant, of a sufficiently different form as to determine it as a different type of duty. This he calls an imperfect duty. An imperfect duty is one which does not bind absolutely (Kant, 1997: 270).

It is clear in the case of a perfect duty that it is determined by what is logically possible and thus the duty which emerges is one which we cannot refuse without descending into the irrational. What is perhaps not quite so clear is why, in the end, this is not also the case for an imperfect duty. If my maxim is such that the effect of my universalising it necessarily contradicts my intended end, then we might understand that to continue to act upon it is, by definition, to step outside the rational.

The foundation of rationalism here seems to facilitate the construction of constraints in that it allows us to see clearly actions it is not rationally permissible to carry out. This is, so far, a negative or constraining ethics. It doesn't tell us what it would be our duty to do in a positive sense. If we take our classic example of lying, it is clear from Kant's laying out of the notion of a contradiction in conception that lying is not permissible. Does this then mean I must always tell the truth? There seems to be something of a gap here. While we might argue that there is such a thing as a lie by omission, this notion already necessarily relies on a sense of what would be pertinent to the context. That is to say, not all omitted information would usually be considered a lie by omission. Were this the case, then we would need to all be in a constant process of vocalising our thoughts in a mad cacophony of streams of consciousness. But, on the other hand, the prohibition on lying cannot simply mean that we should tell the truth when specifically asked. Our duty in this regard must lie somewhere between the two.

To understand how Kant develops a notion of positive, rather than negative, duty, a notion of what we ought, rather than simply ought not, to do, we need to remember that Kant's initial focus is on the will. The notion of will contains within it the notion of an end. If I have a will, then there must, logically, be an end towards which that will is directed. If the end towards which my will is directed is rationally determined or chosen, if it is rational to aim towards this end, then, logically, it must be rational for all rational creatures to aim towards this end. Importantly, the ends in question, in order to count as ends, need to be ends in themselves. Many apparent ends can ultimately be understood as means. If it is my will to eat breakfast, while breakfast is the apparent end, as an ultimate end, it appears somewhat arbitrary. Why would I want to eat a regular and healthy meal at the start of each day? Most likely because I want to stay healthy. Why would I want to stay healthy? Perhaps because I want to maintain my life and this perhaps because of my responsibilities towards my family. While in theory this peeling away of reason could go on infinitely, Kant postulates that rational creatures are in themselves ends. This means that my essential reason for action, the end towards which my will aims, may be another person or, indeed, myself. This doesn't mean, however, that rational beings cannot be means towards other ends. But even when they are, they must still be viewed or respected as ends in themselves. Assuming that human beings are understood as, by nature, rational beings, allows Kant to formulate a second (version of the) categorical imperative.

> Act in such a way that you treat humanity, whether in your own person or in the person of any other, never merely as a means to an end, but always at the same time as an end.
>
> (Kant, 1993 [1785]: 30)

Importantly, here Kant is not suggesting that rational beings, or people, cannot be, or even should not be, treated as means. His deduction is that they must always be treated as ends, even when they are being treated as means. You cannot only treat someone as a means to some other goal. You might treat them as the means to another goal but you must, in so doing, also treat them as an end in themselves. When I visit the supermarket and take my shopping to the checkout, I am quite obviously treating the person at the checkout as a means towards my purchasing my shopping. This seems somewhat unavoidable. What is avoidable is ignoring the person and treating them as a mere machine.

If all moral acts must aim at some end, then the ultimate end of moral acts must itself be the ultimate moral concern. We might, without yet positing any content to such an end, call this the ultimate good. In arguing that rational beings are an end in themselves, Kant is indicating that this ultimate good would necessarily be concerned in some way with the preservation, enhancement or perfection of these rational creatures. Kant refers to this as happiness (1788: 93). The ultimate good towards which we have a duty to aim is complete happiness. While this provides us with the possibility of a positive duty, something we ought to do rather than something we ought not to do, it also introduces a real problem with practical implementation. Where I can rationally deduce whether or not my intention is morally acceptable through the application of the universalising scope of the categorical imperative, this doesn't really work with happiness. Happiness is indeterminate. Not only do different things make different people happy but, moreover, it is neither possible to quantify happiness nor to determine when happiness is enough happiness.

From this positing of happiness as an ultimate goal, Kant purports, however, to be able to develop a notion of positive duty. He argues, on the basis of the goal of happiness, that we have a duty to perfect ourselves and that such a duty is rational. Understood on a purely analytic level, this seems a reasonable enough point. If my ultimate end is happiness, then it is rational for me to pursue such happiness and such pursuit is necessarily going to entail my perfection, where such perfection is nothing less than the narrowing of the gap between my current position and my attainment of my goal.

While the point is easily enough made on an analytic level, can it so easily be established in practice? On a simple level we can explore it through the application of the categorical imperative. Say I wished to renege on any responsibility for nourishing my own talents. I could formulate this as follows: I will that all humanity freely renege on the duty to nourish their own talents as they see fit. While this is clearly not a contradiction in concept and, therefore, I can have no perfect duty to reject this maxim, it could be understood as a contradiction of will on two grounds. First, it could be argued that my happiness, ultimately, will be diminished if I refuse repeatedly to develop my talents. Second, given that happiness is the ultimate end, it seems unlikely that a world in which people are refusing to develop their talents would be a world in which my happiness (or theirs) would flourish. This then suggests that not only can I not rationally support the renunciation of responsibility to develop my talents but that I am actually morally bound to develop them, at least some of the time. Moreover, the requirement of universalisation suggests here that I might have some responsibility for others developing their talents too. The question which immediately arises here is, to what extent?

Were I to propose the maxim that a rational person should commit all their energies to developing all their talents, I immediately run into problems. If each person is concentrated exclusively on developing their talents, then we have willed a rather selfish and quite unworkable society. Moreover, it's quite likely that the development of at least some of my talents is going to rely on the work of others, who, presumably, are going to be too busy developing their own talents. And none of this helps me in any way to determine which of my talents I should be nourishing. Should the maxim be understood as restricted to those talents for which I appear to have some natural capacity? And, even if this is the case, how do I commit fully to developing my skills as a ballerina and my skills as a welder? So, as clear as it might be that I have a duty to perfect myself, exactly what this would entail is left somewhat undetermined. This means that this duty cannot be of the perfect type which would require its unwavering application. Rather, what we have here is at best an imperfect duty.

A perfect duty has no exception. An example of a perfect duty would be the one given above concerning lying. Lying fails the test of contradiction of conception and, therefore, gives rise to an absolute, unwavering duty. Renouncing self-perfection, however, only fails the test of contradiction in will and, moreover, displays itself to be a maxim without precision. It, therefore, only gives rise to an imperfect duty. It is not, at least according to Kant, that an imperfect duty is any less binding than a perfect duty – its renunciation still entails contradictions which it would be irrational to endorse – but its bonds are less definite.

What this does mean for Kant is that we have some duty of beneficence. A social duty. While it may not in actuality be the case that everyone else acts in accordance with the maxims we will, in willing in this way, we assume the potentiality of a society in which they do. Kant terms this a 'possible kingdom of ends' (1993 [1785]: 46). This social dimension then finds expression in a third formulation of the categorical imperative:

> act in accordance with the maxims of a member giving universal laws for a merely possible kingdom of ends.
>
> (ibid.)

This third formulation allows us to see quite overtly the applicability of a Kantian approach to something like an organisational code of practice. There are in many respects strong juridical leanings in Kant's approach. His concern can be seen to be very much with the formulation of rules or laws and their necessary rational-moral underpinning. Of course, this comes with the caveat that in the case of imperfect duties and, therefore, in much of our practical experience, the precise law is not always as obvious as it might be in the case of perfect duties. This notwithstanding, we can see how a Kantian framework could be used to determine the basis of a set of rules applicable to a society of rational beings. The problem is that such a body of law would either be essentially vague or merely a matter of consensus. Sure, we can determine rationally that it is our duty to act with beneficence but what is beneficent in any particular context? How does this mechanism work?

7

PHRONESIS

It is perhaps useful here to turn to Aristotle and his conception of *phronesis*. Some two thousand years before Kant, Aristotle proposed an understanding of ethics based largely on the notion of virtue. Like Kant, Aristotle saw ethics as concerned with ends and determined one of the important ends in human affairs to be something like happiness. For Kant, rational beings are ends in themselves. They are so because they embody the rational moral law. Aristotle approaches the issue from a slightly different perspective and sees all action as being directed towards an end and posits that where such an end is an end in itself rather than an intermediary end towards some other end, then this ultimate end is logically what we could call the highest good. If I am a carpenter, to use one of Aristotle's preferred examples, my aim, presumably, is to be a good carpenter. If I am a flautist, my aim is to be a good flautist. As a human being, then, my aim is to be a good human being. Despite arriving here along a different road, we can see certain similarities with Kant's position. For Kant, it is my duty to perfect myself. Aristotle doesn't determine this inclination as a duty, rather he sees it more like a fact of life or simply a logical conclusion.

Importantly, we should be wary of collapsing one approach here into the other. Kant's view is really, in most respects, quite different from Aristotle's. It is through these differences that we can bring ourselves to one of the key problematics in thinking the ethical. Kant focuses on duty, on adherence to the moral law, which we necessarily know as rational beings. From his notion of the moral law, Kant derives a doctrine on virtue, positing that we have a specific duty towards our own perfection, and towards the happiness of others. These two duties can be understood to be more or less derived from the same point. As a rational person, it would be my rational duty to seek to maximise my happiness, which, for Kant, necessarily, or logically, entails seeking to perfect myself. The same logic would follow for my dealings with others. As a rational person, I would seek to maximise the happiness of other rational persons. Central to Kant's whole project, however, is the notion of free will. It cannot, therefore, be my duty to force happiness upon another or to undertake to somehow perfect him or her against their will. Hence, the different emphasis with regard to myself and others.

Aristotle, too, sees self-improvement as a major goal of ethics. For Aristotle, the goal here is what he terms *eudaimonia,* often translated as 'living well'. Whatever we do, Aristotle reasons, we do ultimately in the service of the goal of living well. What, however, does it mean to live well? The examples Aristotle provides as he unfurls his teleological perspective in the opening paragraphs of *The Nichomachean Ethics* already begin to determine an answer here. The end of the art of medicine is health. The end of economics, wealth. The end of shipbuilding, vessels. Clearly, in each of these instances, the activity is assumed to have a certain function. There may, along the way, be subsidiary functions, but the practice as a whole has a single overriding function. Similarly, then, being human has a function and this function must pertain to what it is that makes us uniquely human. This unique dimension is, for Aristotle, rationality. Our animal dimensions we share with the animals. Only human beings have reason. *Eudaimonia* consists in living by reason. Importantly here, the initial question concerns the function of a human life, not what we ought to do. The answer, then, is not that we ought to be or strive towards happiness (*eudaimonia*) but rather that we ought to have had a *eudaimonic* life. For this reason, Aristotle famously argues that *eudaimonia* can only be measured at the end of a life, once the whole can be appraised (2013 [350 BC]: 12).

Importantly too, Aristotle's emphasis is very much on a life lived. Reason may be the defining feature of human life, but that reason still has to be brought into action. While Aristotle may articulate his *eudaimonic* ethics with certain traditional virtues, such as courage, truthfulness, friendliness, etc., just as Kant does, his project necessarily encounters the question of action in specific circumstances. Where the utilitarians can provide a calculator for such moments, Aristotle and Kant appear to open themselves to the incalculable.

Aristotle's answer is what might be translated as 'practical wisdom' – *phronesis*. Aristotle doesn't believe that a theory of ethics can determine exactly how someone should act in a particular situation. The virtues and his notion of following the mean (e.g. between the excess of rashness and the deficiency of cowardice, we find the mean of courage) allow us to gauge a general idea of how we ought to be, but they do not tell us precisely what to do. When I witness the child falling into the raging river, I may very well endorse the principle of the mean and reject both rashness and cowardice, but this doesn't really tell me at which point jumping into the river to save the child is a rash move. Aristotle argues that no theory of ethics can provide the answer here. Ethical theory provides general principles and these are only ever as good as their appropriateness to the situation at hand. A general theory is unlikely to take account of the particulars of any given situation and this likely omission or blindness is likely to cause errors in application. Even when the general theory isn't actually wrong as such, it is still necessarily too imprecise for the complexities of actuality. The error here, says Aristotle, 'is attributable not to the law, nor the law-giver, but to the nature of the case, since the subject-matter of action is like this in its essence' (2013 [350 BC]: 98). The issue is structural. '[A]gents must always look at what is appropriate in each case as it happens' (2013 [350 BC]: 25).

There are three issues with ethical prescription here. First, a set of rules can only address what has already presented itself as a possibility. It can only factor in situations which have already arisen or combinatory variants thereof. The human world, however, is ever-changing and we are constantly confronted by new, unforeseen circumstances or hitherto unexperienced combinations. Such combinations or original contexts by definition could not be accounted for in a prescriptive code. Second, as indicated above, codes or systems of rules are necessarily general whereas real life situations are always particular. No code of practice, however lengthy, could ever contain the detail of actual experience. This then means codes are likely to run the risk of arbitrarily precluding certain actions and equally arbitrarily legitimising others. There is always a danger then of the rule itself precluding the better practice. Third, Aristotle points out that people are all different. It is not only the details of the external circumstance which are likely to vary and manifest as the unexpectable, but prescriptions also necessarily fail to take account of the particulars of the individuals involved and then, necessarily, the particulars of the relationships between them.

Phronesis is the ability to work beyond these limitations of ethical codes. It is the ability to address the necessary gaps in any rules, the gaps which cannot be accounted for in generalising formulae. It is the perceptiveness, the flexibility, the ability to think *in situ*. It is ethical improvisation. Such improvisation would have to be directed towards taking into account the particular features of the present situation, including the particulars of the people involved. This latter would entail not only the overt characteristics or features of the person but also, and crucially, the relationships between them and us and between them and any others implicated in the wider situation.

While in order for law to be law it would have to apply equally to all under its purview, it is the very generality that such equality necessitates that engenders a particularity in the manner in which abstract law is actualised. This is a point Kafka understood well and famously encapsulated in *The Trial* in the central parable 'Before the Law'. K encounters a priest at the cathedral and the priest tells him a story of a man from the country who seeks entry into the law. The man is made to wait before the gateway to the law. Months and then years pass without him ever gaining access. As he is dying, he asks the gatekeeper why it is that in all the years he has been waiting to gain access to the law, no one else has ever come by. The gatekeeper tells him curtly that this particular gate was 'made only for you' (Kafka, 2007 [1925]: 257). Kafka's insight into the unicity of any encounter with the law is crucial here and points to the structural impossibility of collapsing ethics into any prescribed system of regulation. Put in very simple terms, while the law may tell you what you can and cannot do, it cannot tell you what you ought or ought not to do. It cannot tell you when it is right to follow the law or when it is right to refuse the law. And it cannot tell you how precisely to interpret the law. This is the space Aristotle leaves open for ethics and it is a space that might be understood to introduce a difficult tension into Kant's project.

8

LIMITS OF REASON

Where Kant's entire ethical project rests on the notion of a universal moral law which he equates, ultimately, with reason itself, the mobilisation of this universal moral law in the quotidian mess of lived life, as we have seen, means that Kant has to leave the moral law devoid of detail. It is only insofar as we accede to our own rationality that we will find that we are in fact acting in accordance with the moral law. It is universal insofar as rationalism itself is universal but its applications will always be particular and will require *phronesis* as the vehicle or mechanism for the manifestation of rationality at work.

Despite the fact that for many Kant's is more or less the last word in ethics, albeit often with something of an added utilitarian spin, there is a glaring problem at the core of his proposal. Is rationalism really as unproblematically universal as Kant contends? This question may be understood in (at least) three senses. First, does reason really cover everything, in the sense that it can be understood to expand infinitely to all possible encounters or contexts? Second, even if reason could be understood to expand infinitely, is it seamless? Are there not gaps, holes which reason only glides over, but does not fill? And third, is reason really unitary? 'Universal' means 'turned into one'. If reason has been turned into a unity, then does this not perhaps suggest that something has been lost or excluded in the process? Phrased otherwise, for whom or for what does reason function and what other ways of thinking and being are then denigrated or suppressed?

Some of these points are in fact addressed by Kant himself. Towards the end of *The Critique of Pure Reason*, and in many ways implied throughout the text, Kant argues that pure, abstract reason is unhelpful to philosophy, which has always to deal with the world, with experience. Where the model of mathematics, which is often taken to be the purified mode of reason, can function on its own terms, in so doing, it cannot but reduce itself to an internal and isolated system. Operating on its own axioms, mathematics fails on two accounts. It cannot ground itself, as what is taken to be its ground is internal to its own system. Understood as essentially groundless, it cannot offer any real ground to any practical system of reason. How, in what sense, then, can practical reason be understood to be universal?

It is perhaps helpful here to revisit the categorical imperative itself. Both the first and the third forms of the categorical imperative use what we might understand as hypothetical modes. The first version of the categorical imperative subjects each action to the test of a maxim which can be willed as a universal law. Here, crucially, the auxiliary verb employed is 'can', not 'do'. Similarly, in the third form of the imperative, one formulates one's maxim 'as if' one were legislating on behalf of all. What each iteration of the imperative does, then, is to posit an imaginary community in relation to which one formulates one's maxim. The consensus of reason implied by the categorical imperative is not then related to any actual community. For Kant, the emphasis and insistence on the potential over the actual is essential in ensuring the universalisability of the willed maxim. Application to an actual community would not only be practically impossible, insofar as it would require empirical access and verification, but it would also be temporally impossible, insofar as it would be forever out of time, always anchored to a past moment. As essential as it is, however, the insistence on the imagined tribunal of an imagined community cannot but mean that the community posited is the product of, rather than the context of, the actor, the one willing the maxim. For such an imagined community to function in relation to the categorical imperative, we would have to have already assumed the reason by which the actor is operating is already universal.

The quandary here is that either reason is *a priori* and solid, grounded in something unassailable and external to itself, or reason requires the test of practice, of engagement and questioning, in order to be useful in the world. The first point would be necessary in order for us to accept reason as universal and, therefore, independent of any thinker or community of thinkers. The second point would be necessary in order for reason to be practical. The two points are clearly incompatible, the latter suggesting that the former cannot be the case. Added to this, the very reasoning by which we would decide this quandar, must itself already be part of the reasoning in question. Which is to say that there is already no stepping outside of the question. To even assume to ask what is reason is to assume that there is an answer or at least a way to an answer. This way to an answer would have to already itself be subjected to the test of the very reason its pursuance is intended to ground. This, then, leaves no option other than the perpetual questioning of reason. Even if there were an *a priori* and discoverable ground for reason, confirming it would require us each to continuously practise on and re-question it. Kant details this process in a passage from his third critique, arguing that there are three essential maxims which allow the possibility of such reason being attained. We might call these maxims the maxim of unprejudiced thinking, the maxim of broadmindedness and the maxim of consistency.

There is an obvious subjectivism at work in the application of the categorical imperative, both in the sense that it would be necessary for the engagement with reason to be undertaken by each thinker or party and in the sense that the community imagined in the construction of the maxim is just that; imagined. This internality or subjectivism is entirely in keeping with the first maxim of Kant's process to reason, the maxim of unprejudiced thought, which states that in order to think ethically we must of necessity think for ourselves. To not think for oneself is to think passively, which would then be to open the way for prejudice in one's thought. This is meant quite literally, in that received thinking would necessarily result in the repetition of an antecedent judgement. While there is clearly a retreative aspect here, Kant's point can be understood as a mere logical point concerning the possibility of communication. The less we speak for ourselves, the more we reduce the possibility of communication in that by effectively becoming the vessel for others' thoughts, we reduce the spread of interlocutors to the point where, if we are both or all reading off the same sheet, so to think and speak, there is nothing really to render us distinct. It is only when we truly speak for ourselves that we secure the distinction between interlocutors which guarantees something worthy of the name communication. As noted, the point here is not so much to suggest that this is somehow right or desirable in any utilitarian sense. It is more to make a purely technical point. If we are speaking from exactly the same dogmatic position, then we are not really communicating at all.

As logical as this point may appear, it raises two seemingly opposing questions. Kant seems to be pointing to the possibility of an interlocutor somehow authentically occupying or finding an identity in his or her discourse. At the same time, he is warning against the dangers of mere repetition, warning against the dogma of pre-scripted thought which would be indicative of a lack of any separation between interlocutors. The question then arises as to whether either of these opposing extremes is actually possible. In relation to the question of authenticity, is it really ever possible to 'think for yourself'? All thought, all discourse, is derived and any utterance is necessarily the product of preceding discourses. This is not necessarily to say that new possibilities, new combinations or new ideas do not arise and are not expressed. Of course they do and of course they are. But it might suggest that establishing separation is not nearly as straightforward as Kant is suggesting. On the other hand, we might also ask whether the absolute lack of separation Kant is talking about is ever itself really a possibility. Even when in engaged in internal dialogue there is still, well, a dialogue at work. I am never as simply identical with myself as Kant's concern might suggest.

Another way of understanding this matter might then be to suggest that we are in fact divided – separated, not only from each other, but also from ourselves – by language. The point might then be usefully reworked to focus on the discourse rather than on the speaker. Where discourse is reduced to a unity, without dissent or variation, then there is no communication as such. This changes the point from a focus on the necessity of thinking for oneself to the necessity of ensuring always a polyphony of discourse. This is also then to question the nature or conception of subjectivity operating here. The implications for the thinking of subjectivity and the centrality of *how* we think subjectivity, to this whole matter is something to which we must return below. For the moment it is sufficient to draw out the point that this division of language, the vessel or structure of reason, poses a devastating problem for the notion of consistency.

In the second maxim, Kant goes on to advocate thinking which aspires to breadth not narrowness in perspective. Kant's concern here is to ensure that our thinking is not simply closed in on itself but can somehow grasp itself within the wider context of the debate. Clearly, there is no available vantage point above or outside of human discourse which we could somehow occupy and from which we could look down upon the perspectives of others as well as our own. Such a position is simply not a possibility. The only available means of attaining a true breadth of thinking is as Kant puts it, to 'think from the standpoint of everyone else' (Kant, 1987 [1790]: 174). This again, is a point concerned with communication. Where the first maxim describes the impossibility of communication where there is no variety of discursive positions, this second maxim draws attention to the fact that without striving to grasp the perspectives articulated by one's interlocutors, there cannot be anything which would be deserving of the name communication. There would be mere noise. Communication requires another, as well as an agent.

Clearly, there is some tension between these first two maxims. In order to think for oneself and yet open oneself to the other requires a dynamic process whereby one simultaneously puts oneself outside of oneself, in order to grasp and truly consider the position of the other and, at the same time, one retreats to oneself to ensure that one is authentically thinking for oneself. Kant's third maxim intensifies this tension by stating that one should not only think for oneself while remaining open to the other, but one should also maintain consistency in one's thought. This, by Kant's own admission, is the most difficult of the three maxims to which to adhere. Kant refers to this third maxim as the maxim of reason itself (Kant, 1987 [1790]: 175) and we can see how it is central to our concern here.

If, as we have seen, reason requires mobilisation, actuation and application in order to be discerned, then, despite the fact that it is assumed to be static and transcendentally impervious, it still, in practice, and in order to function for us, can only be understood on the basis of the preceding two aspects of the process; thinking for oneself and thinking in the place of the other. This implies an intersubjective dimension to establishing reason which might be understood as a corrective to the seemingly unchecked internalism or imaginary dimension of the categorical imperative. If the categorical imperative can only function through appeal to an imaginary tribunal, and the imaginary dimension of such an appeal already must assume the universal status of reason, then the process of attaining reason as laid out in the *Critique of Judgement* might be understood as the means by which such reason might be grasped. It is, however, necessarily a fragile grasping.

In the context of the *Critique of Judgement*, Kant is seeking to distinguish taste from reason. Taste would be that inclination which precedes any communication or need for communication. That I feel drawn towards the music of Miles Davis and feel repelled by the music of Elgar is not, at this level of feeling, a matter for reason and consequently not really a matter for debate. It is an opinion and can, as such, be neither right nor wrong. At the point I wanted to debate the matter, I would necessarily have to move into the realm of community and communication and here I depart from taste to reach towards reason.

However, insofar as what I am taking to be reason is only ever what *I* am taking to be reason and I can only recognise the other as reasonable insofar as they are reasoning in a manner commensurate with my own, we might rightly question the extent to which we have really sailed that far from taste at all. This is not merely to make the point that we are inclined to uphold our own perspectives of tastes and find 'reasons' to bolster them. It is rather to suggest that the two operations, while occupying different levels of thought, actually mirror each other in terms of their structure. Just as taste is subjective, so too might be reason, at least insofar as it is mobilised and applied. It is, however, precisely against such subjectivism that Kant is trying to defend. The very basis of the categorical imperative as an ethical mechanism is its universalism. If such universalism is necessarily imagined, not actual, then the imperative starts to slide back into the very subjectivism Kant seeks to avoid. Here we should be careful not to unproblematically equate subjectivism with egoism. The concern here is less with intention and more with exclusion. Where the egoist would serve his or her own needs, the subjectivist merely constructs the means of adjudicating from their own perspective. However eager they are to act for the other or with the other in mind, they are always likely to exclude that of the other or the other's interests which does not fit with their grasp or surmise of the situation, context or world.

Effectively, we are returned to the same point. Without an external or objective determination of reason, we are always in danger of construing reason in such a manner as fits ourselves. The three maxims of the process towards reason are precisely formulated to guard against this eventuality and it is really the third of the maxims which achieves this, albeit through something of a sleight of hand. The third maxim, which ostensibly entails the liberation, or the maintenance of liberation, from superstition, is equated with enlightenment. It is, Kant warns, all the more difficult to achieve when one is intent on stretching one's grasp of the world, of encountering and seeking to understand the new. It is also something, we are told, which can only be achieved through the combination of the maxim of unprejudiced thought and the maxim of broadmindedness and, moreover, it can only be achieved after observing these first two frequently and to the point of habit. And what is it that is achieved here? For Kant it is reason itself. But in referring to it earlier as the maxim of the consistent way of thinking, is Kant not quietly introducing the elusive measure or ground of reasoning which would have to have already been operating in order to support the reasoning he is executing and advocating? The point here is not to argue against Kant's equation but rather to draw out its analytic nature. Essentially, Kant has had to encounter his own axiom. You could argue that Kant's system prejudices against other 'forms of reason' which do not adhere to the principle, such as dialetheism, the view that a statement can be both true and false, in the same sense, at the same time.

While, in a sense this is true, it is perhaps worth pausing before unduly laying into Kant here. While it is fashionable to rebuke Kant for his ratio-centric perspective (Cottingham, 1998), it is important to distinguish the application of Kant's thinking from its grounds (Braidotti, 2006: 14). The point Kant relies on in his argument in *The Critique of Judgement* is nothing more than an appeal to the principle of non-contradiction. While this might be understood as the ground of a particular form or system of reason, due attention to Kant's argument ought to alert us to the fact that it might also be understood as the ground for a particular mode of communication. While it is arguable that there are other forms of reason such as dialetheia, such forms of reason necessarily rely on a different mode of communication. Even this 'necessarily' is perhaps assuming too much. From the perspective of a mode of reasoning which would endorse the principle of non-contradiction, it would seem necessary for a contradictory mode of reason to require a mode of communication which similarly endorsed the compatibility of opposites. Obviously the contradiction suggested here may not be a concern for the dialetheist. Which is then to underscore the point about communication. While it is conceivable that different modes of reasoning exist, it is difficult to see how anything approaching communication between these modes might occur. This then raises the question of whether, within a rationalist, non-contradictory mode of reason it could make any sense to extend the meaning of reason to include something external. Other ways of thinking no doubt do exist but it's difficult to see in what sense they might be termed rational. In order to appear comprehensible to those adhering to a conventionally rationalist discourse, any other discourse would have to similarly eschew contradiction and thus would performatively at least, if not in terms of its content, have to endorse the very thing it sought to argue against. Of course, a contradictory argument against the principle of non-contradiction isn't entirely contradictory – and it would appear to be rather irrelevant whether it was or wasn't – but it is a breakdown in communication, a point of impasse.

The point here is neither to insist on the *a priori* universal sovereignty of (non-contradictory) reason nor to advocate an abandonment of reason and the insistence of a relativism of rationalities. The point is to question the universality of reason as a knowable entity. To argue that reason is reducible to taste is simply to advocate, without reason, an anarchy of thought, a babel of contradicting perspectives with no means by which to adjudicate between them. At the same time, however, insisting on an *a priori* common practice in thought, while simultaneously insisting that the rational is not self-evident, seems itself to be a contradiction. At best there appears to be a circularity here. Kant's three maxims taken together describe the possibility of achieving reason but at the same time the very means by which this reason would be achieved – i.e. rational communication – already supposes the rationality which would be its end. The resolution to the seeming contradiction or circularity in this process is, arguably, precisely to see it as a process. Reason is not self-evident and thus requires the assumption of some ground, such as the principle of non-contradiction, in order for it to be a possibility at all. Seeking to apply this principle then requires communication, but such communication can only function on the basis of this shared, albeit assumed, ground. That not everyone would necessarily adopt the grounding principle is the price that would have to be paid to aspire to the possibility of reason at all. At the end of the day, you cannot have what would appear, from the inside, to be a reasonable discussion with someone who refuses the very principles of the system of reasoning you are adopting. There appears to be no real way out of this deadlock. The only solution, weak though it may seem, is, arguably, tolerance and respect for difference.

By this line of reasoning, it would seem that the universalism of reason, the possibility of creating a unity of reason, necessitates a limit. It is a universalism in the sense of erecting a boundary rather than in the sense of being all encapsulating. Which is also then to say that the universal status of reason, which is required in order for us to pursue or partake in a rational ethics, is at best fragile. It may well be that in order to engage in a rational discourse we have to concede to a grounding principle of non-contradiction but we need also to be aware that this concession is a concession, not a given fact. Insofar as this is the case, we need then to be aware both that what we build on this ground – in terms of our concern here, the ethics we build, justify and endorse – is similarly not given, and not only not given, but not grounded in the given, and that there are other modes of thought which are not only external to our reasoning but which are excluded by it and from its consideration.

I have discussed the above in terms of an inside and an outside which is arguably already, perhaps necessarily, to discuss it in the terms of, and assuming the logic of, a particular way of thinking. However necessary this way of approaching the point may seem, it also serves to illustrate something of a crucial Trojan horse in our argument. The idea that there are some who would accede to a rigorous rationalism, and some who would not, is already predicated on a certain idea of the individual: as contained, as separated, as fully conscious and as itself already non-contradictory. It may well be that our discourse needs, for certain processes, to be rational, in the sense of adhering to the principle of non-contradiction. It is less evident that this mode of thinking is appropriate for everything and really quite evident that this mode is not a mode of being. The human is not inherently rational and the idea of the individual which springs up around this idea is clearly an invention. It is thus an invention of which we need to be wary.

The question of reason's limit, in this sense of its stretch, can be seen through consideration of a famous example Kant gives in *The Critique of Practical Reason*. In discussing the question of free will, Kant asks us to imagine two scenarios. The first concerns a man faced with, as Kant puts it, the opportunity to gratify his lust, with the caveat that once he has done so he will be hanged on the gallows conveniently, and presumably off-puttingly, located outside. The second scenario concerns the same hypothetical man asked to bear false witness against an honourable man with, again, a gallows erected nearby on which he will be hanged should he refuse to do so. Kant easily assumes that, in the first instance, the man would undoubtedly contain his passion and forgo the opportunity for pleasure. In the second scenario, although Kant is canny enough not to assume that the man would necessarily refuse the command to bear false witness, we can at least entertain this as a possibility. Kant's point is to demonstrate the fact of free will. Even in the face of death, we are capable of exercising free will and electing to do 'the right thing'. Kant's explicit point here is that it is through the moral law that we can come to understand the fact that we possess free will. The first scenario is presumably intended to illustrate that our instinct of self-preservation happily curtails our pleasure, thus indicating our unfree 'choice'. In this scenario, we do not act freely, we only 'choose' life because we are by nature inclined to do so. This then allows the second scenario to stand in some relief, illustrating how free will enters the scene and we can actively choose to do the right thing, overpowering our instinct for self-preservation. What is interesting here is Kant's unquestioning assumption that we would in fact refuse the object of our desire when confronted with the assurance of certain death the moment we had finished. Is it not at least feasible that we wouldn't refuse our desire, as irrational as this choice might seem? Certainly, when the threat of death is a little less certain or a little less immediate, many of us do act as though we are happy to accept it as the pay-off for various pleasures. Does not the government health warning on a packet of cigarettes function a little like the gallows in Kant's example? And yet, there have been many it does not appear to deter. And are not, for example, extreme sports enthusiasts precisely accepting or even stipulating death as potential pay-off for pursuing their pleasure? The point here is that Kant's comparison works on the assumption of a particular conception of rationality. For Kant it would be rational to at least consider refusing to bear false witness while it would be irrational to the point of unthinkable to take one's pleasure in the first scenario, knowing one was to be hanged immediately after. The first scenario can be understood in strict utilitarian terms. The pleasure the man would attain from satisfying his lust is unlikely to measure up to the various pleasures he would experience were he to continue living, added to which the pain of being hanged would have to be subtracted from the pleasure. The calculation clearly points towards the choice of renunciation.

The fact that we do, with no small frequency, confound such a calculation, the fact that Kant's comparison does not really work, points to one of two conclusions. Either the rational calculation through which we would supposedly unquestioningly choose life and the ongoing addition of pleasure is not the only form of reasoning available or the choice made here is simply not rational. Either way, the example demonstrates a limit to reason. Either reason is not a unity or it is not uniformly applicable. Human life, human action is, much of the time, not in fact governed by reason or it is not governed by a universalisable reason. It is not that some are rational and some are not, it is that we are rational in certain ways, in certain contexts, and are decidedly unrational in others.

Again, in the context of seeking to apply a supposedly rational ethics, the application of which could be assumed to be universally rational and acceptable to an imagined community, we necessarily encounter a limit to this rationalism. When supposing to imagine the community of reason who would accede or not to our maxim, we necessarily exclude those who do not conform to our own reason. For some, as obviously for Kant himself, the man who finds that, rather than being curtailed by the threat of death, his lust is actually intensified, is simply not rational. But we likely find that the unrational occurs more often than we might at first think. In conjuring an imagined tribunal, we conjure a version of what we consider to be rational fellows but in too quickly following Kant here, we neglect to consider that we exclude a massive dimension of ourselves in this process. It is not simply that we exclude the other – although, no doubt we do – it is that we exclude the other in *me*.

We have already seen how the impossibility of a singularity of reason brings us to the solution of tolerance. We can now add to this the solution – and problem – of responsibility. Returning to the idea of ethics then, in formulating any instance of the categorical imperative, one must first assume the ground upon which one is to do so and then, subsequently, one must conjure an imaginary community of companions in reason. The categorical imperative, which suggests the possibility of a neutral mechanism for determining the ethical, does nothing of the sort. Whatever is concluded remains, as does the grounds on which it is based, the responsibility of the one who concludes it.

9

AGENCY

Already through the notion of free will discussed in Chapter 8, Kant is resting on an idea of the human subject as responsible in the sense that they are the ground of their own actions. For Kant, as for many others, the whole project of an ethics, or even the whole concept of ethics per se, already relies on some notion of free agency, of an agent who acts as the ultimate ground or decision point for their actions. If your actions arise on the basis of a cause outside of yourself, if your actions can be reduced to prior effects, then it is difficult to see in what sense your actions could be construed as ethical. A machine functions without values. It is difficult to see in what sense a machine might be ethical.

Taking this as read, the notion of responsibility with which we are concerned here must be a notion of responsibility which contends with but also moves beyond the first sense of being responsible for, of being the *prima causa* of, one's actions. Clearly, recognising such responsibility might figure as an important aspect of ethics, in the sense that without acknowledging oneself as the cause of one's actions, one could be accused of refusing charge of what one does. To adamantly refuse any volition might even be understood to be an absurd position insofar as one could never own the very renunciation itself. Between these two extremes, however, it is conceivable, and no doubt a highly frequent occurrence, that people are rather selective in discriminating between the actions for which they would wish to see themselves as responsible and the actions they would prefer to see as arising from some other cause beyond their control.

Psychology itself has a peculiar role to play in this distinction and serves further to highlight the problem of the simplistic division a Kantian approach assumes. For Kant there are simply two possibilities in terms of causation. Either something follows, in some chain of causes, from natural law – for example, the famous apple falling from the tree – or it doesn't follow from natural law, in which case it must have been caused by spontaneity, meaning it must have arisen as a result of a free willing agent. This free willing agent arises as a logical necessity precisely in the context of seeking – that is, assuming the need of – a *prima causa*. If we work from the assumption that all states emerge on the basis of natural laws governing preceding states, then either we have to accept an infinite regress or we have to assume some sort of independent base of some initial intervention. The infinite regress cannot work for Kant as it is simply an ungraspable idea. A series composed entirely of subordinate moments but no beginning is rationally unthinkable. What Kant famously occludes in this move is the possibility of something arising by pure chance. The aleatory does not exist for Kant, neither as a first moment nor as an intervening force. This means then, that for Kant, every event, every change in state is caused by an initial deliberate move. Working back from any change of state, we may have to follow a series of chain reactions before arriving at the initial deliberate move or the two may connect immediately.

Leaving aside this question of the aleatory for now, Kant's schema slides quickly into the reductively subjective, the idea that where there is no prior cause, the spontaneous cause, which remains the only alternative, must sit with a willing agent. This is to then root the very possibility of undetermined action to the faculty of reason. All actions outside of nature arise through reasoned thinking and decision making.

What this underscores is the essential link between the conception of ethics and the conception of the agent or subject supposed in this conception or supposed to be acting in this conception. How you think or imagine the agent, person, subject, actor etc. (clearly the term one chooses to use here already tips one towards a particular notion) who might be said to be acting or being ethical already begins to shape what such an ethics might be, or sets limitations on the scope of what might be understood as possible. Kant's argument around free will might be understood to be fundamental here. Without free will, it could be argued, there is simply no possibility of the ethical at all. Without free will, without the choice to act in this way or that way, it might seem absurd to begin to ascribe any sort of ethical value to an act or to judge the actor as having behaved ethically or been ethical. To echo a famous phrase of Nietzsche's, a tree does not choose to be a tree, does not choose to grow this way or that. It would seem absurd then to credit the tree with having chosen to grow in the right way.

Related to this, and central to Kant's project, is the question of motivation. It is not simply that the notion of free will already implies a certain motivation, but, moreover, that any such motivation would also need to be accessible. If Kant cannot establish the possibility of free will, then he cannot establish the possibility of motivation. Even if he can establish the logical possibility of free will, which would then imply motivation, without knowing what this motivation is, it would seem too much to impute any ethical value to the action which followed. Kant is quite aware of this himself and insists that motivation is key to the moral law. Any action which is undertaken for what he terms pathological reasons, whatever its outcome, is not compatible with the moral law. What Kant is less adequate to answering is how anyone might discern this motivation. The apparently obvious answer here would be that while one's motivation for acting may not necessarily be discernible to others, it is still known to the one who is acting and, therefore, only limits ethics in the sense of social accountability. In this understanding, you may not know whether or not I acted ethically, as you cannot know what motivated my decision to act. But I know. Arguably this could be understood as a key distinction between ethics and law.

The question Kant needs to answer, however, concerns the extent to which one can actually access one's own motivation. To what extent, that is, am I actually transparent to myself? As Freud rather pithily pointed out in the opening lines of his *Ego and the Id*:

> To most people who have been educated in philosophy the idea of anything psychical which is not also conscious is so inconceivable that it seems to them absurd and refutable simply by logic.
>
> (Freud, 1923: 13)

Freud's point most obviously evokes the Enlightenment turn in philosophy, a perspective perhaps most commonly gathered under the proper name of Descartes and his famous *cogito,* in which consciousness and the very existence of the self are posited as conterminous. It is, for Descartes, only insofar as he is engaged in conscious mental activity that he can be said to exist at all. Insofar as psychology can be understood to be a Cartesian discipline, this problem of limiting the psychical to the conscious could be seen to go for it too. While it would be unfair to suggest that psychology refutes any possibility of non-conscious mechanisms, it nonetheless appears to hang itself on its own uncertainty where it vacillates between, on the one hand, asserting the necessity of non-conscious aspects to the mind, without which it – psychology – appears rather redundant and, on the other, insisting on the self-efficacy of the human agent who is rendered equivalent to its mind. If the mind is reducible to conscious activity, then this would be to suggest that the activity of the mind is transparently accessible to the actor or subject in question. If on the other hand the mind is not reducible to conscious activity, then this suggests that there is something, even much, of the mind which is beyond our (conscious) control. Retreating, in what we might not unfairly characterise as horror, from the Freudian implications of a psychical force beyond our control, psychology appears ever more drawn to neuroscience, and to the endeavour of finding its answers in the mechanics of the brain. The paradox here is that this shift towards neuroscience is much more the death knell of psychology than psychoanalysis ever threatened to be, insofar as it appears to exclude the mind entirely.

An example of this contemporary neurophilosophical perspective would be that advanced by Thomas Metzinger in his *Being No One*. Metzinger quite clearly argues, as his title already suggests, that the idea of a self is really nothing more than that: an idea. In claiming that there is no such thing as a self, Metzinger's point is not a million miles away from Hume's famous notion of the bundle self. Hume bases his argument on the logical fact that in order to have an idea of something, we would need to have had an impression or experience of it. There is, however, Hume argues, no experience or impression of the self. What we experience, rather, are various separate impressions. Moreover, these several experiences are in constant flux and cannot, therefore, be taken to ground something invariant and substantial. In fact, Hume argues, the idea of the self could be understood to arise precisely in response to the inconstant experience of experience. Speaking from a quasi-psychological perspective, Hume draws attention to the manner in which we subjectively or phenomenally translate variation into a supposedly seamless unity. It is, he suggests, as a side-effect of this process of synthesis that we 'run into' the idea of a self (Hume, 2003 [1739]: 182). The idea of the self is an after-effect of an inability to function in a world of flux.

Echoing some of these points, Metzinger argues that what we call the self is nothing but a special kind of representational content which he calls the phenomenal *self*-model (Metzinger, 2003). This phenomenal *self*-model is composed of those aspects of one's being in the world to which one can direct one's attention: physical sensations, emotional states and cognitive processes. While we might then term this congregation of impressions the self, this is only ever a metaphorical move. There is, Metzinger insists, no *thing* here to be named. The phenomenal *self*-model, as Metzinger's cognitive terminology might suggest, is nothing but a process. This process cannot be considered a self in the sense that it is not a substance. There is no thing which lies behind it, which does the 'doing' of the process or experiences the functioning or the outcome of the process. There is just the process and the bodily mechanism, including the brain, which is the vessel for the process. Metzinger is comfortable with the existence, and apparently the entitative existence, of biological organisms. Some such organisms are subject to phenomenal experiences and some such phenomenal experiences can give rise to the idea of having a self. The fact that we phenomenally experience ourselves as substantial, essential and entitative does not actually mean that we (noumenally) are substantial, essential and entitative. The problem for human beings, in this regard, is that while we experience the phenomenal representations which give rise to the idea or illusion of a self, we do not and cannot experience the representing function which lies behind this process. For the most part, we encounter only the outcome, not the process itself and it is this limitation which leads us to error.

In a manner not dissimilar to Hume's, Metzinger's model here brings to the fore the relational nature of phenomenal experience. Hume had based his argument against a substantial self on the fact of the illusion that where there is experience of something then there must be someone or some discrete things having that experience. What this argument promotes then, albeit it perhaps subtly, is the idea that preceding the, albeit mistaken, establishment of a self, there must be relating. Hume appears to assume that in order for us to allow our varied and inconsistent impressions to lead us to imagine a self which experiences these impressions, we must encounter something which is other. In this picture, not only is the idea of the self illusory, but it is also, of necessity, secondary. It would not seem to be possible to encounter an idea of the self without having encountered (an idea of) something else.

Metzinger clarifies this point through the idea of an emergent relationality through which, he argues, ideas of objectivity and subjectivity emerge together. The emergence of the phenomenal experience or illusion of the self is in this sense part of a wider process through which a relation between the organism and the world is made possible. The phenomenal *self*-model may, then, be nothing more than a model or a metaphor, but it is an essential idea insofar as it allows the possibility of cognitively processing a range of relational conjunctions, not only with the environment and things in the environment but with comparable others and with oneself. The very possibility of an organism relating to its own physical and psychical properties in a manner which takes them as being in some way homogenous rather than heterogeneous is, according to Metzinger's argument, predicated on the perception of separation which is facilitated by the illusion of selfhood. It is only on the basis of an idea of the self that one can begin to grasp an idea of context and, at the same time, it is only on the basis of an idea of context that one can begin to grasp the idea of a self. To think that I perceive myself, I have to think that I perceive myself in some sort of relation or, more likely, in some sort of complex of relations to the world around me. Such contextualisation functions as a primary conjunction of self and other. In the idea of me *in* the world, the conjunction of the preposition covers over the co-poietic emergence of the assumed parts as already distinguished. In simple terms, this integrates the possibility of world and consciousness at a phenomenal level.

Not only must a conscious being experience a world in which they experience themselves, but it is only insofar as they are conscious that they can do so. We might understand the body in this picture as the liminal aspect of the self-world relation. Typically, and in a Cartesian heritage, the self is construed as something distinct from the body. At the same time, our commonsensical grasp of the self would be such that it entails the body as a peripheral, though not inessential, aspect. Distinct and yet implied. There appears to be an element of indecision here. We identify with the body and yet we are reluctant to predicate identity on the body. Part of Metzinger's project appears to be to upend this hierarchy. For Metzinger, what is, is the body: the biological, empirical substrate. The self merely functions in relation to the body as an epiphenomenal effect. What is crucial for Metzinger is, then, that self is not something which simply exists or, to echo Sartre, precedes existence. We might even say it, the self, is not something which really exists at all. This is clearly the sense of the title of Metzinger's magnum opus, *Being No One*. The self ought to be understood to be an effect, an idea. But it is not an actual entity as such.

What we need to remember, however, is that in Metzinger's model, just as the self is not a reality as such, but rather a phenomenally presented construct, so too the body, in Metzinger's system, can only properly be understood as a construct, as an idea of body. The self is presented as a functionally necessary effect which is experientially 'housed' within a body which is then experienced as its liminal extreme. This body, though, can itself only be known as a phenomenal entity. The body, which is taken to house the phenomenal experience of the self, which is assumed as its substrate, can lay claim to no more reality than the illusional effect it is taken to ground. In order to function at all in the world we must create an idea of a self and we must create an idea of a body which would pertain to this self. Empirically speaking, the body and, as a part of the body, the brain would necessarily take precedence and we can easily start to understand the self or mind as construct, a convenient or functionally necessary operation of the body or brain. However, this empirical starting point has to be properly understood to be an idea and, therefore, yet another convenient and functionally necessary assumption. Put in terms of a possibly inappropriate spatial metaphor, the phenomenal self (mind) emerges as an insubstantial idea within the physical organism of the body, which itself emerges as a construct within the mind (phenomenal self).

Where then does this leave us in terms of the question of agency? Are we not returned to Nietzsche's deft dismissal of Descartes, when Nietzsche argues that Descartes was trapped unknowingly in grammar and the assumption that behind any activity, such as thinking, there must exist an agent (Nietzsche, 2002 [1886]: 17–18). Agency, or the existence of a self as an agent, for Nietzsche is nothing but a habitual but erroneous assumption. We do not act. We do not choose. We are, rather, moved and the assumption, the idea, that it is we or indeed any *thing* else that has caused this is simply an illusion. If the self does not exist, however, how can we retain any notion of autonomy? And if autonomy is not a possibility, does it make any sense to continue to talk of ethics?

Despite refusing the substantiality of the self, Metzinger seems, curiously, to retreat from this Nietzschean conclusion and opts rather to maintain a fidelity to the notion of autonomy. What then might be the agency of such an autonomy?

The *auto* of autonomy would suggest the idea of an agent who would direct themselves. An agent in this sense, then, would be one which is not restricted to the effects of nomothetic reverberations, but can itself initiate. Conventionally, such autonomy might be understood as the ability to rationally control one's actions and might usually be taken to imply an ability to control or form one's own convictions or will. That is, autonomy would usually suggest a freedom and a directive ability in terms of (aspects of) one's inner and outer world without such freedom ever being understood to be total. I may choose to raise this glass of water to my lips but I cannot choose to fly, although I can imagine myself doing so. With autonomy, while I cannot necessarily control the environment in which I find myself nor the others by whom I find myself surrounded, I can exert some control over my own movements within this environment, my own engagements with others and I can affect, to some degree, my own thoughts. Autonomy, then, is always limited autonomy. We can see then how autonomy can be understood not only to span inner and outer experience, but also that it entails two conceptually distinct if not unrelated dimensions. One's autonomy is limited to the extent that one is not free from nomothetic determination or from environmental or social restraints. In addition to this, one's autonomy is limited to the extent that one does not determine one's own direction, either internally or externally. Assuming we have an ability to choose, to determine our own courses of action and thoughts, our own interests and preoccupations, we could understand that autonomy also then entails the ability to will what we become. We are autonomous to the extent that we can shape ourselves as well as our own destiny. You can change your diet, give up smoking, take up running, just as you can learn Mandarin, study Renaissance art and practise meditation. You still can't learn to fly, although you might dream you did. But who or what, if any*thing*, is the author of your dream?

The interior dimension of autonomy can be understood in a number of distinct ways. On perhaps the simplest level, one can control or affect one's focus of attention. This might include consciously shifting one's attention from this book to the television and back again. It might include electing to ignore the dentist's drill as it penetrates your root canal. Perhaps most illustratively, it would include the shift involved in seeing a face and then a vase and then a face again in the famous Rubin Vase. In each of these examples, we can imagine that the autonomy is perhaps limited but this is not to say it is non-existent and, clearly, the extent to which it is will be different for, and will be experienced differently by, different people. One can also experience control of the steps of one's thought. In solving a problem, we appear to determine solutions or options. In reminiscing, we walk through past events in what presents as an order of our own choosing.

The Rubin Vase is an illustrative and simple example to work with. Looking at the image and focusing your attention on the two profiled faces, you can easily, through a conscious, mental shift, 'lose' the two faces and 'find' a white vase. It seems evident that there is a choice at work here, a moment of decision and control which feels perceptible. You could even say that in the experience of the deliberate shifts of attention that the Rubin Vase invites, you can directly experience yourself as agent. Compare the conscious experience of something like the Rubin Vase and the everyday experience of completing habitual tasks wherein you might easily lose awareness of the process you are engaged in. You leave the house. You lock the door. You walk away only to have to return, unsure whether you actually did lock the door or not. The two experiences are markedly different. It is not only that in one you are aware whereas in the other your engagement is buried under the routine and repeated nature of the task. In the experience of the Rubin Vase you feel yourself present, you feel yourself active, whereas in the locking of the door you are somehow absent, inactive, despite the fact that your body is clearly engaged in performing the act.

It is important here to distinguish a number of potentially confusable conceptual elements. In an everyday idiom, one could easily collapse autonomy into agency assuming along the way that such autonomy would by definition entail conscious, rational control. That is, as with Kant, autonomy not only appears to imply rationality but rationality, in order to be enacted, implies autonomy. The logic here would be that in order for a process or activity to be understood to be rational, it would need to be understood to be (freely) elected. Somewhat counter-intuitively then, this suggests that computers do not function rationally. This would not be to say that they are irrational. It would simply be to say that they are not, in and of themselves, rational. A calculative process can be understood to be logically constructed but for something to be actively rational requires the exercise of reason which is a freely elected engagement. At the same time, in order to be understood to be freely performing an action (including the action of thinking), you would have to be understood to be following rational principles. The problem with this logic is that it is unavoidably Ouroboric. If proceeding rationally requires that I proceed according to preset principles, then it is difficult to understand in what sense the actions or thoughts which follow on the basis of this could be said to be entirely free. If they cannot be understood to be free, in the sense of freely chosen, then it is difficult to understand in what sense it is me that is being rational. The rules may be rationally or logically structured but this does not mean that I am being rational in following them. It is only when I can be said to be electing to act that it could be me that is said to be rational. The rational agent has to in this sense exceed the principles or system which would confer rationality upon him. Put paradoxically, there must be an unrationality to being rational. There needs to be a moment outside of reason which allows a rational process to be understood as rational rather than simply machinic. This is the significance of the distinction Derrida (1997: 68–69) draws between a decision and a calculation. A calculation merely follows preordained schema but it can never account for the initiation of movement.

An impossibility seems to insist here. Either we are effectively programmed, sent down a track which has already been laid for us, or our intervention, our initiation, is always a moment of madness which cannot be accounted for within the system of reason which would allow us to describe it as rational and, therefore, free. Either we are not free because our rational path is set or we are not free because there is no rational path.

Nietzsche perhaps best captured this issue when, railing against Kant, he contended that in order to be understood to have free will, in order to be understood to be autonomous, one would have to be *causa sui*, one would, in his evocative image, borrowed from Baron Münchausen, have to have 'pulled oneself up into existence by the hair, out of the swamps of nothingness' (Nietzsche, 2002 [1886]: 21).

What can be easily missed in Nietzsche's image of the self-raising swamp-exiter is that its apparent absurdity rests upon the paradoxical assumption of the reality of the swamp of nothingness itself. To create the idea of the impossibility of pulling oneself into existence out of the swamp of nothingness by one's own hair, the image might be understood to subtly rely upon the idea of the possibility of exiting the swamp in some other way. Of course you cannot pull yourself out of the swamp by your own hair. This contravenes fundamental physical laws. You could, however, pull yourself out of a swamp using a conveniently placed vine securely attached to a nearby tree. Except, however, the swamp of nothingness, in order to be the swamp of nothingness, would have no vine, no tree; it would have no thing. The conveyance of the impossibility of self-raising, of self-creation, appears to rely, in Nietzsche's formulation, on the contradictory assumption of a preceding reality. This, it must be stressed, is not the point to which Nietzsche wishes to take us. His aim is to reject not only the notion of free will but to reject also the notion of an unfree will. The problem with free will, for Nietzsche, might be understood to concern the idea that this free will is somehow a personal possession. This problem then goes equally for the reverse. Will (in general), for Nietzsche, is what presides, not the agent who would be (mis)taken to be the agent of this or that will (mistaken as a particular).

It is not, then, that Nietzsche is seeking to simply refute the obscene logic of self-causation but he is seeking to challenge the conventional notion of causation itself. Where causation might be understood to already imply a notion of agency of some sort, a prime mover, Nietzsche wants to posit will as the agentless cause of all. What we might conventionally characterise as the human agent is clearly not, then, for Nietzsche, something which moves itself, which determines itself. It does not enjoy autonomy, at least not as we have defined it. We are subject to various drives and it is the manner in which these drives are played out that determines 'our' course of action, our lives. The person, as such, plays no active part. We are moved. We do not do or choose the moving. Whatever we experience as choice is but will in action. In this sense, the idea of pulling oneself out of the swamp of nothingness should not be compared, in your imagination, to the idea of being pulled out of the swamp of nothingness by someone or something else. Only will moves us. It is the entire image which is illusory. There is never a swamp of nothingness from which we could extract ourselves. The self is, rather, a by-product of the force of will.

Will, as a general force, might be understood to manifest in the human being in the form of drives or desires. In a turn of phrase which might be understood to echo or continue the metaphor of the exit from the swamp, Nietzsche argues that 'we cannot get down or up to any "reality" except the reality of our drives' (Nietzsche, 2002 [1886]: 35). This might be understood in a similar way to the problem of the hierarchy of body over mind endorsed by Metzinger. In Metzinger's argument regarding the phenomenal *self*-model, we will recall that the phenomenal self only exists as a notion, an idea, even an accident. For Metzinger this accident is housed or occurs within the only properly existing reality, the empirical world of which the body (and thus brain) is a part. But we needed to add into this picture the fact that the empirical world including the body can only appear to us itself as a phenomenon and thus cannot be accorded a reality 'above' that of the self. Nietzsche's hypothesis is that it is will – the force of the drives which constitute our only reality – which might allow the possibility of our grasping the world as party to the same reality. What Nietzsche is contending here is that we are driven by the same will as everything else in the world or, phrased otherwise, everything else in the world is driven by the same will as us. Will is the one cause, the 'only type of causality there is' (Nietzsche, 2002 [1886]:36). This being the case, all life, all movement, all process emanates from this one singular force, what Nietzsche famously terms the *will to power*.

Remaining with the metaphor of the swamp, we might imagine that for Metzinger and his adaptive argument, the human animal could most probably be traced back to some progenitor crawling out of the primordial swamp, driven by evolving instincts, a will to survive. Conceptually, this doesn't seem so far from Nietzsche's point. The individual appears ineffectual and ultimately unimportant. A mechanism is at work, a will, a power, which infuses everything.

In Nietzsche's understanding, what moves us are drives, multiple drives. At any moment our existence is beset by different, opposing drives. You may want to eat the chocolate you bought earlier. At the same time, you may want to lose weight. You may want to go to the gym but at the same time you feel inclined to go to the pub. All the time, you know you have work to do and, hard going as you know it will be, you do want the rewards successful completion promises. Conventionally, we might understand that in order for there to be a possibility of deciding between these different drives, there must be some sort of supervening *I*. We might call this the self or the intellect or perhaps the subject. Nietzsche's solution is, arguably, rather simpler. Nietzsche suggests that what decides between the different drives operating within us is simply the drives themselves. One drive overrules or dominates the others and it is this which leads to a certain action taking place rather than another. That I do end up working rather than going to the pub or gym is explained by my drive to work being, ultimately, stronger than my drive to exercise or socialise. Our inclination to identify with the stronger drive is merely a convenience, a seduction. We are no more the victorious drive than we are the defeated drives, a point perhaps attested to by the fact that the drives continue and their interplay is not consistent. The drive to work which wins today may be defeated by the drive to drink tomorrow. I will inevitably find myself in each in succession. The impression of an agent of choice is itself nothing but a drive manifest. That often it might be the case that a sense of guilt extends my struggle or tips me to one inclination over another is perhaps illustrative here. If I am nothing but the dominant drive, then why or how can a defeated drive exercise guilt over 'me', who is the object of guilt and why would the defeated drive not simply remain defeated?

It is simple enough to perform the intellectual trick of a shift in perspective and, as it were, zoom out to consider life on earth as an impersonal, unfolding, mechanical process. If we consider a virus rather than the human animal, we circumvent or believe ourselves to have circumvented the problem here insofar as we relinquish an attachment to ownership. We want to see, we are accustomed to seeing, human life as impregnated with meaning, with deliberation, choice, consequence and value. With a virus, on the other hand, we are much more accepting of the notion of life happening to it. The progress of a virus may be understood to be regulated and a virus may even be understood to be self-assembling (Zlotnick and Mukhopadhyay, 2011) but we would not, or not usually, think of the virus itself as intending its assemblage. We can, that is, all too easily accept the idea of life being governed or determined by a force greater than the individual to the extent that the individual barely counts at all. Is it then simply the case that an adherence to the idea of something like a self with something like a free will is mere fancy, a vain belief which functions to cover over our impotence and inevitability?

One problem with this position is that it seems already to turn back on itself. A question insists here. Assuming that the substantiality of the self, and thus, necessarily, its freedom, is an illusion, then we might ask, for whom does this illusion function? This is not merely to rehearse a Cartesian position and to assume that where there is a doing, there must then be a doer. From a Nietzschean position the fact that there is a belief in a freely willing self does not in any way suggest that there is a substantial believer believing this belief. Neither is it to pose the seemingly perfectly reasonable and, again, Cartesian question as to why an impersonal force would need to conjure the impulse for us to insist, erroneously, on our own solidity. From a Nietzschean point of view, this question is moot. It wouldn't require reason. What is in question is arguably more fundamental and allows us to glimpse the incompleteness of the illusory-self position.

Kant had already encountered this issue and, arguably, he already had an answer. What distinguishes us from the virus, on this question, is the matter of apperception. Where Metzinger appears to separate the self from the substantial substratum of the body, according the latter a reality and explaining the former as a phenomenal occurrence which emerges from or as an effect of this reality, Kant introduces what we might understand as a third dimension. It is Kant who posits the distinction of noumena and phenomena upon which Metzinger builds. The noumenal world must exist, Kant argues, but equally it must remain inaccessible. The only thing we have access to, he argues, is our phenomenal reality, or reality as it appears to us. Put very simply, the only way I can know the world is through my knowledge of the world. This clearly includes my knowledge of what I would take to be myself. Kant's *I*, however, is reducible to neither of these concepts. Kant's *I*, that is, is neither the noumenal substratum nor the phenomenal self with which I identify. Where Metzinger wants to stand on the ground of a firm reality from which he can admonish the Cartesians and their assumption of a core-self, Kant allows a more radical and more rigorous perspective. The difference between the phenomenon of the body, the body as it appears to us, and the mind, what Metzinger calls the phenomenal *self*-model, is that the former is assumed to be underpinned by a noumenal correlate whereas the latter is what we might understand as a pure phenomenon. What Kant sees, and Metzinger appears to miss, is that the point of perception of both these phenomena cannot itself be reduced to either of them. That is, something else must insist, something beyond both the phenomenon of the material body and the phenomenon of the self. Neither presented as a phenomenon nor assumed as pre-present noumenon, this something can only be understood as a purely subjective emergence.

The *I* is situated, then, as the necessary counterpart to the phenomenal *self*-model. But it is not merely situated in the convenience of the passive voice. It can only be properly understood as situating itself. The danger here is that of falling back into the assumption of some sort of substantial entity. If the self and the empirical reality are accessible only as phenomena, then the *I*, the subject, risks coming to be understood as the one substantial reality. This misses the point. It is not that the *I* is anymore attainable or experienceable than the phenomenal *self*-model. In fact, you could say it is less experienceable. The phenomenal self model may not exist as such but this never stops it being experienced. The *I* on the other hand is never experienced and cannot be demonstrated but rather must be posited as a necessary unaccountable moment. It has to be inferred through its own absence. It can neither be experienced nor proven but it must be assumed in order for those things which are taken to be experienced or proven to be entertained as possible. It is in this sense that, contra Nietzsche's gibe, pulling oneself up into existence by one's hair out of the swamp of nothingness is precisely all one can do. The 'impossible' act at the centre of Nietzsche's image, is in fact the only possibility.

Part of the problem here is that in order to think this problem at all, we are necessarily always already *in* the problem. This is not only a problem of context but, a fortiori, a problem of time. In ridiculing the possibility of *causa sui*, Nietzsche is borrowing a scene attributed to Baron Münchausen wherein the Baron, having stumbled into a swamp, is able in defiance of the laws of physics, to pull himself out by his own hair. In empirical terms, the tale is obviously fanciful, another tall tale from the *Lügenbaron*. This is presumably Nietzsche's point. It is unbelievable. As ludicrous as the scene is, however, it does, in order to maintain its point, its preposterous nature, rely on a conventional or commonsensical chronology. This is more easily seen in the original story where the sequence of events follows a commonly acceptable structure. The Baron stumbles into a swamp where, in order to save himself, he seizes himself by his ponytail and raises himself, and his horse, to safety. We should not forget, however, that the form of the story is *mise en abyme*. The Baron's adventures are always being posited back from a point narratively prior but chronologically subsequent to the events being related. The Baron presented as the narrator of the story, who is already a fictional or fictionalised character, is always distinct from the Baron depicted in the action narrated. When Nietzsche borrows the image, what he appears to neglect is the complex time suggested. In mockingly proposing the image of someone raising themselves out of nothingness, Nietzsche neglects the retroactive dimension which might be applied in *causa sui*. It is not so much that I, at some finite moment in the past, when previously I didn't exist, created myself. It is rather that I will always have posited myself. I will always have been in the process of positing myself on the basis of nothing other than the fact of my having been positing myself.

A similar point needs to be considered in relation to Metzinger. His vision in which the neurophysical substrate gives rise to an illusion of selfhood, in the form of the phenomenal *self*-model, appears to assume a quasi-scientific, atemporal perspective wherein what is being described simply *is*. Such an atemporal – and, not unironically, asubjective – perspective, as with scientific perspectives in general, relies on the evacuation of the subject. We see this evacuation most obviously in the convention of adopting the passive voice in scientific writing in order to maintain an appearance of objectivity. The passive, god's-eye perspective on the anonymous, impersonal everyself occludes the fact of the subjective positing essential to the idea being presented. A passive voice may successfully suggest an objective perspective, but it is in action that subjectivity consists.

The issue at stake here is not simply one of ethics but is, as may now be apparent, one of psychology. At stake here is the very possibility of psychology, insofar as we understand psychology to be the study of the *psyche*. It is not simply that, reduced to an organic mechanism, the *psyche* in psychology is lost. Much more significant than this is that such a loss is only ever possible through a sleight of hand which, at the same time, dispenses with the possibility of ethics. Without God, without religion, without some higher or exterior authority, we appear, as we have seen, to lose the possibility of the ethical. Without something upon which we can ground an ethics, it appears to inevitably slide towards a matter of 'anything goes'. At the same time, as we hurtle towards an ever more totalising embracing of science, the need to ground ourselves in the possibility of something certain appears to result in the exclusion of the possibility of volition. Where the activity of the mind is inaccessible and beyond control, it would, at least conventionally speaking, seem problematic to start to impute or ascribe ethical determination to that mind. If it is unknown, then we cannot know how we, or anything else for that matter, might influence it. This being the case, it would seem absurd to assume responsibility or culpability for what emerges. If we are – to follow the neuro-scientific perspective to an extreme – nothing but electrochemical fluctuations, then how can we speak of ethics? If we are but electrochemical reactions, then our actions are determined by our nature, by our physiology. We might push this line of thinking one step further and say that if we are nothing but electrochemical fluctuations and reactions, then it makes little sense to talk of anything like a self at all. The idea that anything meaningful might demarcate one self from another self seems, in this picture, rather fanciful or, at the most, simply a habitual manner of speaking.

These two issues entwine. Without the possibility of something beyond or outwith the organic, beyond the body, beyond the brain, there is and can be no possibility of psychology (at least as anything other than a documentation of mere behaviour, which is to say, psychology without the *psyche*). At the same time, recovering a place for something beyond the physical would appear to be the condition of the possibility of recuperating the something of the ethical. It is not that something like a subjective position can be demonstrated to persist as such. It is rather that, due to the fact of our retroactive relationship with the very question we are asking, we cannot but reinscribe the space of something like the subject. An irreducible gap opens up. This gap is the possibility of the ethical and it is the imperative of a psychology which owns the name. The question is not then, *what am I?* Rather the question is something more like, *what (or who) would I have to have been to understand the question in this way?*

Such self-positing is not merely a question of epistemology, then, but is necessarily already a question of ethics.

10

BEYOND UNITY

Part of the problem here is an attachment to a notion of unity. In thinking personhood, in thinking something like the agent of an action which would be considered to be ethical or not, we tend, habitually, and unquestioningly, towards the assumption of unity. Such a notion of unity haunts proceedings, teasing at the edge of our thinking and forcing the reconfiguration of that which would otherwise appear disunified, that which would otherwise appear contradictory, incomplete, incoherent, fractured. In approaching the disunified, we tend to make it whole and refuse as irrational that which appears unwhole. Psychology obviously plays a part here. Our notion of personhood as atomistic, as reducing to and cohering around a unified core, as manifesting with a constancy, if not always with a manifest consistency, remains a cornerstone not only of our self-conception but, by extension, of our notions of agency, responsibility and thus the possibility of ethics.

Our dependence on a notion, or notions, of unity lead us to an impasse here. That we are inclined to imagine ourselves as being unified in ourselves supposes a separation from that which, both spatially and temporally, surrounds us. This insistence on subjective unity then necessitates a plurality, necessitates a notion of an other from which the subject would be distinguished. At the same time, our notion of a natural world, of which the subject would be a part, obviously occludes the possibility of the subject being other to nature. The advances in neurophilosophy which push towards a machinic conception of human existence do not simply encounter the problems of the experience of the existence of a self, as addressed by Metzinger, or the attendant logical problem, which Nietzsche first draws to our attention, as to the apparent impossibility of thinking a separate, freely self-directing entity with an external root. Where there is an external root, the root maintains a causal tie with what follows. It is this that necessarily leads to the apparently absurd image of the self plucking itself from the swamp of nothingness by the locks of its own metaphorical hair. Thinking human existence in terms of its natural ground appears to close down the possibility of thinking something human which exceeds, which cannot be ultimately reduced to, this natural ground. Which would be to say that thinking the human as something which cannot exceed a natural causal order appears to close down the possibility of thinking the human as subject at all. At the same time, thinking the subject as something excessive in relation to any natural order is to open the question of the origins of the subject. If not rooted in nature, then in what is it rooted? If rooted in nature, then how could it in any part be anything else? The very question here already assumes a unity which must contain the elements supposed.

Core to disentangling this matter is the issue of time. In conceiving of the subject we tend to fall prey to the illusion of externality wherein we situate ourselves in some imaginary point not only outside of the subject but, moreover, outside of the timeline upon which we would imagine the subject. We see, as it were, the subject ambling along through time, tossed and hewn by the events of life and, as we squint, we imagine we can discern a continuity which keeps this subject as this subject, a thread of self, a core unity. The image we construct here seems eminently logical and, in fact, it is in this appeal to logic that it achieves its sleight of hand. Logic legitimises the shift to the abstract upon which the image here depends. The act of conceiving of the subject appears to require an abstraction from experience. The danger lies in the risk of forgetting that this is what we have done and assuming then to treat our abstracted image as real. Paradoxically, in imagining our subject on an abstracted timeline, we appear to have constructed an atemporal subject.

To conceive of the subject from the inside, so to speak, we would have to refuse the convenience of an external vantage point. Such a shift is not, however, a mere shift in perspective but rather entails a radical disturbance of context. Relocated to the perspective of the subject, we lose any clear, measured notion of time as a flat line upon which the subject travels. The subject no longer appears as a stable X which proceeds from A to B but rather the subject becomes the empty space whence both A and B unfold. It is a giddier perspective. In the former, conventional perspective, the subject appears, logically enough, to have its origin in nature, as that is from where it is taken to have emerged. Nature is, so to speak, its point A. In our second, chronologically troubled perspective, this original point A appears as nothing but a projection. Understood from this perspective, the natural grounding doesn't so much precede and determine the subject but rather proceeds from and is determined by the subject. So thought, we begin to understand that the manner in which we conceive the subject tells us much more than mere facts. In fact, the facts don't really factor in this matter at all, insofar as what we would be calling facts are already of necessity elements or products of a particular conception. What remains, however, is the core idea that the conception itself is productive and is productive of a particular notion of subjectivity.

In this way we can begin to understand that the very notion of subjectivity with which we contend always already supposes a notion of something like desire. The very desire to posit, to uncover, to think, to reveal, to construct, to imagine a subject, an idea of what it would mean to be human, of personhood, of self, is what remains. This points then to a radical division at the heart of the subject wherein the subject we conceive always has to account for the fact of its entailing a conception of subjectivity. We might call this fantasy.

We conventionally think of fantasy as a staged scenario, a more or less consciously constructed alternative reality in which we enact or receive those things we feel unable to enact or we are unlikely receive in real life. But whenever we engage in such fantasy, there sits behind the overt, staged fantasy a certain idea of ourselves. This certain idea needs to be understood on a number of levels. Not only does the fantasy we project for ourselves illuminate our, often hidden, desires but it projects a notion of who we would be in the scenario of confronting, achieving or receiving those desires. In order for this agental idea of our fantasy self to emerge, we must first have an idea of what it would be to be a self at all. That is, before – and the 'before' here should be understood in the sense of logically before rather than chronologically before – before we ever get to the specifics of me, albeit fantasy me, we must already have an idea of us, what it means to be a person at all. This more generalised notion is likely to be informed by various experiences, from overt education to more indirect sources such as media, upbringing, culture, religion and experience. There is necessarily a looping effect here too where the notion of self we harbour already mediates, filters and determines our experiences before those experiences go on to shape the conception of self we hold and so on, in an ever-circling loop wherein each repeatedly reinforces the other. We can imagine that in such a reinforcing loop, alternative conceptions or contrasting ideas, challenges to the existing – though never quite finally sclerosed – model are not going to be well received. We may accommodate what we can of them but if they present as too alien, we will no doubt shun them, disparage them or simply fail to recognise them. In this sense our core fantasy becomes largely sealed in on itself. It is ever becoming hermetic and self-supporting. What doesn't fit the model is rejected. What already fits the model is taken as evidence that the model is robust.

Never quite distinguishable from this abstract notion of selfhood we find our own particular idea of ourselves. In many ways this personal vision might be understood to be the original from which the more general notion is derived. We emerge as sentient beings rather preoccupied with our own existence, our own plight, even as we don't yet have the capacity to configure our relationship with ourselves in this precise way. Narcissistically driven, we shape the world around us in our own image even as we shape our own image on what seems closest.

Our temptation is to posit a starting point, a point of origin here. Is the self, that which is most intimately me, the original from which I generalise an abstract being? Or is it in encounter with the abstracted shape of being that I begin to model myself? Is it through recognising myself in the other and then another other that I can come to generalise a wider we? If so, then what grounds the initial recognition here? Surely in order to recognise myself in the other I would already have to have recognised the other in myself. But such obsessing with origin is only an artefact of the external god's-eye view we assumed, the distant vantage point from where we imagined ourselves travelling smoothly from *arche* to *telos*.

Thrust back into the fact of life, we discover again that there is no discernible starting point. The very idea of a starting point, and then the particular content of that starting point, and then what preceded that starting point, is only ever retrospectively posited from some later point. Retrospectively and retroactively, for it is never simply a case of looking but also always a case of shaping.

We stare into the mirror and we imagine we encounter ourselves as we are. But this is not possible. We think ourselves and think we are thinking ourselves as we are, but this is not possible. At the very least, in either of these configurations, there are two. The image which confronts us when we turn to the mirror is never us. Ignoring the obvious fact that it is but a distorted and inverted reflection of light from a polished surface, it is necessarily partial in three important regards.

Except for the relatively rare experience at the hairdressers, few of us ever encounter the back of our own heads. The mirror image with which we are familiar is the frontal view and even here it tends to be the top portion of a frontal view. Even faced with a full-length mirror, most often our attention is drawn up to the face. The image you take from the mirror, then, is not an image of you but rather an image of a part of you: the front of your head.

Even on those rare occasions when we are afforded a view of those odd bits of us which usually escape, the bits other people see all the time, we are still only encountering the reflection of a surface. The mirror image has no interiority. On a purely organic level, it is not composed of organs as we are. It doesn't pump and gurgle with the flow and process of life. It doesn't feel, doesn't ache, doesn't tingle, doesn't pang. It is, by definition, superficial.

Added to this, as an image it is only ever taken in and, in being taken in, it is subject to a necessary preselection. We isolate elements of the image, focus on certain parts over others. We interpret the image and organise what we see according to our expectations of what we would see. Just as we filter all reality, so we filter the image of ourselves we meet in the mirror. Such filtering then becomes not simply selective but also constructive. We manipulate, impose, occlude, assemble, foreground. We, as it were, pull ourselves into existence out of the mirror of nothingness.

In encountering this partial, mediated, assembled surface image, I mistake it for myself. The surface, being only a surface, a screen, is ready to reflect whatever it is I project onto it. But no matter what I project, the image cannot but remain other. Something alien in the image resists my grasp. Try as I might to coapt the image, to make it fit my idea of me, something always resists. It is other. The very fact of the partiality of the image means that it can never be adequate to my lived experience. As I stand before the mirror, there is necessarily an inequality between my experience of myself and the image I see before me. With no interior dimension, no commentary, no narrative of its own, it seems perhaps less complex, less conflicted, less concerned. In this sense it cannot but appear more complete, more coherent. The inequality quickly emerges as not simply one of difference but one of antagonism.

This moment, this encounter with my other self, my self as other, is a continual process, an ongoing moment. Unsettled and unsettling, the otherness in and of my self-encounter demands a solution. And so we turn to fantasy. Or so we have always already turned to fantasy. The incohesion of self-experience gives rise to the notion that it could be otherwise and this then is the core of all fantasy, whatever the subsequent content. The core of fantasy is the idea that it will, somehow, all be all right in the end, that there is a sense to it all, that I somehow fit, that I am, that I am something after all and that this something that I am has a place.

We imagine, then, a self which is ultimately self-sufficient and thus self-enclosed, even if so often this self-enclosure takes the form of a conjunction with or even dependency on others, and perhaps, particularly, on a particular other. In the fields of love and sex, which are not accidentally central here, we seek union and imagine that such union will bring completion. But the honeymoon period always ends, bringing with it another other, ostensibly the same person but never quite the same as the mis-take you first fell for. In a not dissimilar way, in the field of consumption, we imagine possessing that which will render us complete; a new pair of shoes, the latest technological gadget, a new home. The scenario of obtainment deflation is familiar. Giddy with the expectation of finally getting your hands on that hitherto elusive object of desire, you wait those final moments as the shop assistant processes your payment and packages your item. It is in your grasp and you turn to leave the shop and with each step the elation declines, the object diminishes in value. Its fading power may last until you get it home, may even last a few weeks, if you are lucky. But sooner or later, the once mesmerising object of your desire will have become another bit of tat. We are all King Midas in reverse. In shopping as in love.

Alejandro González Iñárritu's 2014 film *Birdman* offers us an unusually expanded example of not only the multiple divisions produced here but also the crucial fact of there being no 'true' accessible position beyond or before these divisions. The film focuses on the plight of an ageing actor, Riggan Thomson, who had once enjoyed great success playing the titular character in a comic book adaptation franchise. Determined to return to his theatre roots and re-present himself as a 'serious actor', Riggan decides to stage an adaptation of Raymond Carver's (1981) short story 'What We Talk About When We Talk About Love'. The preparations do not, however, go terribly well. Days before opening, one of the lead characters is injured on stage. His replacement is an established, revered but arrogant and opinionated stage actor who quickly begins to destabilise an already wavering production.

Much of the action in the film takes place in Riggan's dressing room, where he sits before, and thus doubled in, a mirror. On the wall behind him, and thus constantly reflected in the mirror, is a poster from his earlier film, *Birdman*. The figure of Birdman thus literally looms over him, lending a rather obvious metaphor of how his past as Birdman continues to dominate how he is perceived, and in this way haunts him. Sitting, ostensibly alone, in his dressing room, Riggan begins to hear the Birdman berate him. The Birdman then appears in the flesh, as it were, chiding and coaxing Riggan, referring to the two of them as 'we' but, keeping in mind that the superhero was played by Riggan, the 'we' here is always also an 'I'. Always also or almost. There is neither one nor the other but rather a perpetual teetering between.

Beyond this relationship with Birdman, the film can be understood in terms of the various relationships in which Riggan finds himself. There is his lawyer, producer and friend Jake, who appears as the voice of reason and thus anchors Riggan to a manageable social reality. There are his ex-wife and daughter, who puncture his self-image with home truths and, particularly in the latter case, scathing alternative reflections of who he might be. Similarly, the new addition to the cast, the more critically successful and younger actor Mike Shiner (the star!), challenges not only Riggan's decisions, ability and understanding of theatre production, but most crucially, his self-image.

The film begins with a poem, 'A Late Fragment', from Carver's posthumous collection, *A New Path to the Waterfall* (1989), which sets the focus for the film. The poem concerns what we might understand as a perspective on the value or meaning of life, positing that value as the fact of being in the position of the beloved. It concerns, that is, reflected identity. Life, according to Carver, is about recognition in the eyes of the other. Riggan's very existence depends upon, is defined by, the manner in which he is seen by others. Which is to say, then, that he is defined by the version which is reflected from those around him; from the ageing cinema-going public who would remember him from his *Birdman* days, to the theatre critic poised ready to destroy him for what she feels he represents, to his own family and their various emotionally framed perspectives. Amongst these various Riggans reflected from others, conventional wisdom suggests we find the real Riggan and this is how many have read the film. He, the real Riggan, remains at the core of the story, simply losing his mind and imagining an implausible

superhero figure following him around, the superhero being assigned
the role of superego, imagined or metaphorically represented as an
external interlocutor. We easily acknowledge the core self because we
are accustomed to acknowledging the core self. Even when the core self
seems not to be present, we see it there. We struggle to accept a version
of the story – any story – where the core self simply doesn't exist. Where
things begin to fall apart, where a stable identity doesn't obviously
emerge to hold the narrative together, we still assume the necessity of
one and suture proceedings together through appeal to insanity.

What this conventional reading of *Birdman* occludes is the fact that
performance lies at the heart of the film. The very fact of performance,
without any substance behind it. Like Shakespeare's *Hamlet* or Raspe's
The Surprising Adventures of Baron Münchausen, the film is *mise en abyme,*
structured with a play within the film which echoes or mirrors key
aspects or themes of the framing narrative. Where some use of *mise
en abyme* merely repeats, and thus draws attention to, core thematic
aspects, the play within *Birdman* properly mirrors the concerns of the
film, which is to say that, like a mirror in reality, it does not merely
reflect what is before it, but rather, in the process of reflection, it
distorts, inverts, selects and obfuscates.

The play, like the epigraph, is from Raymond Carver and, like the
epigraph, it concerns the idea of self and self-identity enmeshed in
and reflected from others. The play is an adaptation of Carver's short
story, 'What We Talk About When We Talk About Love'. The original
published story is set around a kitchen table and, more specifically,
around a bottle of gin, and has two couples relating stories which weave
together various perspectives on the idea of love. What is revealed in
the successive telling of the stories is an idea of identification on the
part of the teller. Each character finds themselves reflected in the story
they tell. Or, perhaps better said, each character develops and projects
an idea of themselves through the story they construct. Each character
becomes an idea they have of themselves through the telling of the
story of love they imagine as reflective of themselves.

Curiously, the two core stories within Carver's narrative are
concerned with what we might understand as a failed unity. A sense of
love as union, a romantic notion of love as refinding can be discerned
on the surface of the stories. The wife's story of her ex – a dependent
abuser who tries and eventually succeeds in killing himself when
she leaves him – is told in terms of an irrational, unbearable love, a
love which is too strong to allow the lover to survive. The wife, as

the beloved, is aggrandised in her relating of the tale and it is difficult not to read her current relationship as somehow lesser in comparison: more sane, more stable but less intense and, therefore, as entailing less love. The husband's tale doesn't overtly concern himself but an elderly couple he encountered in hospital. After a road traffic accident, the badly injured couple are trapped in body-casts. Although they are in the same room, the husband, it transpires, is deeply distressed because he can't see his wife. The body-cast means he can't turn his head. He is physically close to her and yet immeasurably distant. Again, a romantic notion of love is suggested here. Love as union. Love as unity. Or love as fantasy. Which is to say that what the story presents is a story within a story where the diegetic stories rub uncomfortably against the extradiegetic story. The characters, as the title suggests, talk about love but what they say when they talk about love tells of themselves and the distance between themselves and idea of love they talk about, the difference between the idea they have of themselves and the idea they would have of themselves. The key to this difference appears to lie in the imagined presence of another.

The careful revelation in Carver's layering is accented further in *Birdman* where the stories are conveyed within a play within a film. Supposedly finding a point of imagined identification with Raymond Carver, who had apparently left him an encouraging note on a napkin after a childhood performance, Riggan determines to adapt, direct and star in his own version of Carver's story, refracting himself through layers of identification: with the author, with the character and with the abusive former husband, the character within the story told within the play.

What we might understand as the romantic notion at the core of the Carver story is upended through Iñárritu's refusal of any stable point of perspective. Where romantic love points towards a one, another understanding of love might be one which points towards a plurality. This other notion of love would be what shatters our compulsive narcissism and draws us outwards. But then what emerges from Carver, at least in Iñárritu's hands, is the idea that the precarity of love is both a cause and a consequence of our paranoiac recoil from the other. Paranoiac narcissists spun on an impossible axis of self-negation, we are temporally out of joint, always too late to quite grasp what we might have been. Through the layering of narrative levels, Iñárritu's film denies the audience any fixed context from which to properly grasp Riggan or from which to ground a diagnosis of insanity. This is the point many viewers of the film appear to have been drawn to, that

Riggan is obviously, through the course of the film, losing his already rather fragile mind. The film, however, might be more productively understood as a complex and layered presentation of the impossibility of the self. Many critics of *Birdman* were wrong-footed by the ending, where Riggan's daughter enters his hospital room only to find an open window and her father gone. Jumping to the obvious conclusion that the broken man must have committed suicide, she goes, sadly, to the window. She looks down, but clearly sees nothing and then looks up and smiles. This ending obviously doesn't fit with the realist narrative of a failed actor gone mad. It suggests rather that the Birdman was real. Or suggests that there is no Riggan. This, arguably, is the point of the film. It is not that we are somehow inauthentic in our being in the world and thus need to excavate our true selves. We are image, we are cloaked in the protective armour of a false identity, in the mask and suit of our fantasy, but with nothing behind it. This is the experience of self, however else we want to cover it.

If the experience of self, and what this would come to mean, is already steeped in multiple layers of uncertainty, then this poses a number of unavoidable questions for psychology. To even raise the question of what the experience of self would come to mean is to raise a tangled complex of questions. What can we know or say about the self which would be taken to have been, whether at the core of experience or somehow as that experience itself? And then what would be the significance or ramifications of this fact of experiencing? While it might seem logical to assume that any uncertainty in the former will cast a shadow of uncertainty on the latter, the reverse temporal logic with which we are constrained to approach this means that this is only the case insofar as the uncertainty is felt. The 'insofar' here, however, is no simple matter. Where demonstrable certainty is unavailable, which is clearly the case when it comes to the self, then one might still retain a(n undemonstrable) belief in the experience of the self or the self of experience. Such an undemonstrable belief is, obviously, what we would call faith. This seems to bring us into some sort of (quasi-) religious discourse. It is ironic then that this appears to be the refuge of a discipline ever eager to present itself as grounded in hard and fast truths. Of course, the uncertainty of science is well-known and well-accepted. Not only does the impossibility of epistemological certainty pull the rug from under empiricism every time, but the structure of knowledge itself is such that experiential facts must always be framed in terms of theory. It is not simply a case of being locked in an infinite regress of asking, as Lyotard pithily put it, 'what proof is there that my proof is true?' (Lyotard, 1979: 24). The nature of human knowledge is such that what is known can only be known in terms of a linguistic framework which would mediate the first-hand experience of that which is taken to be known. There is necessarily an irreducible gap.

The term 'experience' comes from the Latin *ex*, meaning 'out of', and *periri*, meaning 'to go through', suggesting that experience is that which you must go through and come out of. The thing *experienced* cannot, by definition, even be understood as an experience until you have been through it and come out of it. The thing experienced cannot be experienced in and of itself. It can only be experienced, turned into an experience, can only come to be understood as an experience, once it has been left behind. You cannot occupy an experience. To be understood as an experience, the thing experienced, what we might call the material of experience, must be turned into an experience. What we can convey of experience, even to ourselves, is only ever a version of that which was experienced. What we go through is fashioned, transformed and turned into expression, into words. Experience must be inscribed. And so inscribed, so worked on, experience can never pretend to certainty.

11

NEGATIVE CAPABILITY

The poet John Keats, in a letter to his brothers, in December 1817 coins a curious term: *negative capability*. In the letter itself Keats defines this notion as the state or habit of being 'capable of being in uncertainties, Mysteries, doubts, without irritable reaching after fact & reason' (Keats, 2009: 41–2). By way of illustration, he names Coleridge as one without such capability. Coleridge would, he says, be 'incapable of remaining content with half-knowledge' (42). For 'a great poet', he continues, 'the sense of Beauty overcomes every other consideration, or rather obliterates all consideration' (42).

At the centre of Keat's concern here appears to be the notion that the 'great poet' ought to be able to – or, perhaps better, is defined in terms of their propensity to – resist the urge towards certainty, towards closure. The implied reasoning here is straightforward. Absolute certainty is impossible and, therefore, clinging to the possibility of this impossibility is not only contradictory but necessarily entails the endorsement of illusory ideas. Subscribing to pre-existing doctrines closes down the possibility of *seeing* or *grasping* experience.

Importantly, though, all experience in order to come to be understood as experience must be mediated in language. This is not a straightforward chronological process either. It is not simply that we move from something like raw experience to a mediated containment of what has been experienced. Rather, what we would call direct experience itself is always already inaccessible and beyond our reach. It is not that we emerge from experience into language so much as we are already encased in language. This notion is not new and has been described in various ways for centuries, in vastly differing traditions, by mystics like Ibn 'Arabi who presents a concept of the real which is knowable only as shadow but in itself remains immeasurable and endless, or even by Kant and his notion of the transcendental object or thing-in-itself. As different as these two thinkers may be and as different as the details of their particular configurations of the beyond may be, the core sense of an internal obstacle to certainty remains.

The phrasing in Keats's letter, however, is somewhat less than clear. The position of negative capability he wants to endorse is simultaneously articulated to half-knowledge and to a sense of beauty. While there is nothing to suggest that these are mutually exclusive, it is not immediately apparent how they might relate. The idea of a potent sense of beauty appears to suggest a highly subjective perspective which is echoed and supported elsewhere in Keats's letters where he writes of 'the authenticity of the Imagination' (34) and how such truth is seized in beauty rather than through 'consequitive reasoning' (303). The opposition here would suggest that, for Keats, emotional and imaginative intensity are the key to negative capability. What is important to grasp here, however, is that such emotion is emotional engagement and such imagination is imaginative response. Despite appearances, Keats is not advocating solipsistic subjectivism. Neither is he simply extolling the virtues of a conventional artistic leaning. Beauty for Keats is not a given and is not a matter of convention. And truth or authenticity is clearly not something which can be understood without the conjunction with and activity of the one who would conceive it. Beauty, however, is not purely or exclusively in the eye of the beholder. And nor is truth something which can be merely conjured. What Keats appears to be pointing to is a specific mode of interaction with the world, one which respects both the impossibility of unmediated experience and the impossibility of isolated self-sufficiency. In another letter from a few months after the negative capability letter, he contrasts the image of a honey-bee and a flower. The bee, in Keats's description, is active and purposeful but in so being, the bee is determined in its activity and its life by a 'knowledge of what is to be arrived at' (63). The flower, on the other hand, is patient and passive and, crucially, receptive of the unexpected, 'taking hints from every noble insect that favors [it] with a visit' (ibid.). The key here is that the flower is not merely susceptible to the machinations of its visitors but rather takes hints from them. Hints, not truths or answers.

Two important points emerge from Keats's analogy. First, there is the upending of the hierarchy between bee and flower, between a simple conception of activity in opposition to passivity, of production in opposition to reception, where the former term in these related pairs is automatically valued over the latter. It is not that Keats is suggesting a reversal but rather a dismantling wherein the assumptions underpinning the opposition no longer hold. '[T]he receiver and the giver are equal in their benefits' (ibid.), he tells us.

Second, there is the complex matter of certainty and, particularly, how we might or can respond to the reality of uncertainty.

The slide of psychology into a branch of applied statistics might be understood to be one response to this matter of uncertainty. Observational science, which is one way of understanding or describing what it is that psychology does, is marked by certain limitations. That this observation may at times entail observation under experimental conditions with the factor observed being a delimited variable which is taken to be dependent on another, manipulated, variable, while adding further not unimportant limitations, does not dispel the base nature of the operation: that of observing. Of the limitations which present themselves here, two are worth highlighting. Whenever some event or phenomenon is observed, there must be an observer and an observed. This would appear to be an analytic truth of the notion of observation. If there is no one or no thing doing the observing, it makes no sense to say there has been an observation and, similarly, if there is (absolutely) nothing to observe it is difficult to see in what sense an observation can be said to have taken place. As asinine as these points may be in their obviousness, there is an element of the latter point which perhaps needs to be articulated. If the act of observation depends on something being there to be observed, then equally, the act of observation pertains only to that thing and not to other things which remain unobserved. The second limitation is that when such observations take place, they necessarily take place in the past.

As simple as these limitations might prove to be, they are stark. While a discipline like psychology might have productively occupied itself with the practice of observation, detailing particular perspectives on particular occurrences at particular times, it chose not to. Instead it enlisted statistics to enable the expansion and generalisation of the phenomena observed and, crucially, the prediction of future phenomena. So determinedly did psychology step over this line – a line between past and future – that this has come to determine the very identity of psychology. Psychology is that discipline which allows us to predict how people will respond, perform, behave ... maybe even think (although, curiously, this latter appears to have become less and less of a concern for psychology). The question then is how it might be possible to cross this line from past to future. While psychology may have decided that this line has already been crossed to the point where it is churlish to think further on it, in reality, the line has to be crossed again and again each time an experiment is conducted, results are generated and conclusions drawn. Each act of quantitative psychology which purports to say something about people (in general), rather than *those* people (specifically), requires a recrossing of this line. The question, then, is how is this possible? Or perhaps, simply, is this possible?

The obvious answer is that statistics provides various tools for determining probability. Applied to the idea of either a wider, different or future population, the operation would be as simple as determining the probability of *x* recurring in said population. Probability works rather well with simple factors. What is the probability of rolling a six on a standard die? To calculate this you simply divide the number of events, the number of rolls of the die, i.e. 1, by the number of possible outcomes, i.e. 6. So you end up with a probability of roughly 0.167 or 16.67 per cent. What such a simple calculation of probability relies upon is the fact of there being a totalisable number of possibilities. Such number of possibilities can be immense and need not even be finite, but they must be conceivably totalisable. Put rather simply, in order to calculate probability, there has to be a number of possible outcomes. Where there is no way of conceiving or containing the possible outcomes, then there simply isn't a number. Where there is no number, there is no possibility of calculating probability. As we have known since Cantor, you cannot calculate probability on the basis of an open set. The ramifications of this point are complex and open up important lines of debate in terms of our understanding of the universe but they have a rather straightforward consequence for the study of psychology.

The human mind – what we might understand to be the proper object of psychology – is unquantifiable. It is, therefore, not susceptible to probabilistic calculation. Human behaviour and human responses can be observed. We could even argue that aspects of the mind itself might be observable through mechanisms of introspection or even inquisition – although, obviously, what is being accessed here is far from immediate. But as the human mind cannot be determined – as we have seen, its existence is of the status of necessary assumption – there is simply no legitimate mechanism to infer from one mind to another and no possibility of suturing any such uncertainty through appeal to probability. This returns us to Keats and his notion of negative capability. It would seem that this ability to be 'in uncertainties, Mysteries, doubts, without any irritable reaching after fact & reason' (42) might be understood as essential to any meaningful understanding of what it is that psychology might be and, as a mode of response, then, might shed light on the question of ethics in psychology.

Broadly speaking, it would seem the contemporary psychologist's response to this concern is not at all to sit comfortably with uncertainty. Rather the psychologist, wittingly or not, embraces the surface of the exhortation conventionally attributed to Galileo to 'measure what is measurable and make measurable what cannot be measured'. Rather than confront and continue to explore the human mind, the complexity of that node of experience – that which we experience as experiencing the experience we experience – the psychologist seeks to reduce the object of study to something which appears more measurable. In so doing, the psychologist might be precisely understood to be irritably reaching after fact and reason. The problems in such irritable reaching are manifold but lead eventually to the core of our question.

Where the object of study cannot present itself or be accessed in a quantifiable form, how do you proceed? How do you make measurable what cannot be measured? One might understand, given his area and work, that what Galileo meant was something akin to strive harder, reach further. That is, one might understand there to be a matter of *not yet* implied here. What is not yet measurable ought to be pursued until it can be measured. What such an interpretation doesn't account for then is the question of that which is structurally inadmissible to measurement. Galileo most likely wasn't suggesting that something like happiness or love might be reduced to a universal scale. Whatever Galileo meant (it is doubtful he even said it), attempts have been made to measure precisely these things. The contemporary psychologist, encouraged down the road where measurement is paramount, is faced with the choice to measure the unmeasurable or to measure something else. Ultimately both options here necessitate a similar sleight of hand. On the one hand you overtly shift your attention to something which is measurable, such as reaction times, limited stimuli responses or brain activity, or, on the other hand, you code or translate psychological phenomena in such a way that it can be quantified. The problem in both these approaches is that they end up presenting as psychological something other than the psychological.

This error is most obvious with the shift towards cognitive neuropsychology where brain (in)activity is mapped onto the presence and absence of behavioural responses and reproducible skills. It is not merely that this process illegitimately reduces the human to a mechanical entity but really more problematic is the fact that it reduces it to a normal entity. The reduction to a mechanics is the result of an error in thinking, a failure to grasp the impossible point of experience which, whatever its nature, cannot logically be reduced to the mechanics of which it may or may not be the effect. Neuroscientists, with their studies in brain plasticity, are already aware of this. While there is perhaps something of a levelling uniformity in the reduction of the human to a machine, the assumption that that machine then operates in a uniform manner introduces far greater concerns. The operation of psychology whereby the human is reduced to a norm, where the idea of the normal human is arrived at and subsequently globally broadcast, becomes much more one of production than of description. Somewhere in this process, perhaps inevitably, the terms 'norm' and 'normal' slip from their statistical usage into their juridical and moral usage. In seeking to produce a clean, scientific description of the human psyche, its nature, its state, its functioning, the discipline of psychology must produce a lens, a filter, a mechanism whereby that which is immeasurable becomes measurable, a tool to make a number where no number was. The tools to produce this number, the tools which allow the possibility of this knowledge, then necessarily produce an idea of the human psyche cast in their own shape. Psychological knowledge is far from clean, objective or true. Psychological knowledge is an effect of the forced passage through its own assumptions. And this effect comes to then determine what would be desirable rather than to describe what is.

When Keats sides with the flower over the bee, he is not making a mere fanciful gesture, a romantic posturing of opposition to the predominant preference for the active over the passive. In upending this hierarchy, Keats even goes so far as to make the point that active and passive cannot be so easily separated in cases like these. Keats's real target here is the question of certainty and particularly, at this juncture, certainty directed at or assumed in the future. 'Let us not,' Keats says, 'go hurrying about and collecting honey-bee like, buzzing here and there impatiently from a knowledge of what is to be arrived at' (63). The point here is that the knowledge of what is to be arrived at precedes and thus determines and limits the activity. The bee is motivated by an *a priori* goal. Such predetermination cannot but limit what the future will bring. While planning and goal orientation may seem efficient and admirable, when confronted with necessary uncertainty, such goal orientation is a disabling factor. The openness of uncertainty is closed down by a fixation on 'what is to be arrived at' (63).

Keats's point here would be well heard by many in academia, not least in that most indeterminate of disciplines, psychology. He, Keats, goes on to say, 'who thinks himself asleep' is awake (64). The very propensity towards control, the discomfort of uncertainty, closes down the unknown to come. Targets and a fixation on impact, which, in order to be achieved, will have to, paradoxically, already be defined, are the determiners of contemporary research. This means not only purporting to already know the terrain of the future but endorsing such knowledge with an unequivocal certainty. In this sense, what passes for research – in the proper sense of *recerche*, the act of searching closely or intensely – is nothing of the kind. Rather it is a pre-limited activity of confirmation which, wittingly or not, seeks to contain the uncertainty of the future by painting it in the same colour as an already limited variant of the past.

Curiously, in the midst of his contemplation of the bee and the flower, Keats makes reference to the impossibility of comparing pleasure between the sexes. Just as it would be unsupportable to claim that the bee gains more than the flower, so, Keats asks, 'who shall say between Man and Woman which is the most delighted?' (63). This is precisely the question that was famously asked of the seer Tiresias.

Walking in the hills one day, Tiresias, so the story goes, comes across two copulating snakes. For reasons unknown, he strikes the snakes with his stick. Offended by this, Hera, the queen of the gods, punishes him by turning him into a woman. He spends seven years as a woman, becoming a priestess to Hera, marrying and going through childbirth. After seven years as a woman, Tiresias comes across another pair of snakes copulating and either leaves them be or tramples them (the story is unclear) and, as a result, is turned back into a man. Later, as he is uniquely positioned to provide an answer, having experienced both sides, he is called upon to settle an argument between Zeus and Hera as to who gains more pleasure from sex, the man or the woman. Zeus claims it is the woman. Hera claims it is the man. Tiresias affirms Zeus's perspective and says that it is indeed the woman who takes the greatest pleasure from sex. Enraged with his response, Hera blinds him. Unable to reverse Hera's punishment, all Zeus can do is conjure some compensation. He endows Tiresias with the power of clairvoyance. In some versions of the story of Tiresias, his skill is specifically, much like Daniel Paul Schreber (2000 [1903]), that of augury, the ability to interpret birdsong. What is determined as an indubitable mystical power in one age is madness in another.

Keats in his discourse on negative capability is clearly pointing to the impossibility of certainty and the common discomfort this induces. But he is also pointing to an essential liminality, the structural necessity of such impossibility. Uncertainty isn't a matter of undiscovered knowledge. It isn't a matter of not having yet travelled far enough to find the certainty which has hitherto escaped our grasp. Uncertainty is an effect of the structure of experience. Who can say who gains the most pleasure from sex, a man or a woman? Outside of Greek myth, no one can. Not only does the question suppose that there is already a generality to the two sides (and that there are two sides) but it foregrounds its own contradiction. The question could only be answered by falling on one side or the other. A question which would require the existence of a third position in order to be answered presupposes the division of humanity into only two.

Similarly, the meaning of the future or what the future will bring is structurally inaccessible. In order to access the future, in order to know what the future will bring, we would have to have already entered the future, at which point by definition it is no longer the future. The only way to know the future is to wait for the future to become the past. Even then, as we have seen, for that which has been experienced to be known it must be turned into something knowable. Which is to say, it must be transformed, and then must ever after be interpreted. The bridge between worlds, the bridge between man and woman, between past and future, between possible and impossible, between the experience and what can be said of that experience, may appear mystical but is the function of interpretation, a function embodied in Tiresias. Curiously, in stories in which he appears, Tiresias is renowned for his unwillingness to unveil the future with any great clarity. Rather than simply say what will happen, he talks in riddles. He lifts one veil to reveal another. His interpretation, that is, requires further interpretation. Always.

To some it may seem that it is essential for psychology to play the game of statistics. Without making this move, it cannot say anything apparently meaningful about wider or future populations. In order, however, to submit to the mechanisms of probability and generalisation, in order to utilise anything other than a purely descriptive statistics, and say something apparently meaningful, psychology must partake in two crucial moves. It must make a number of that which has no number. And it must submit to a process of conferring meaning on that which, on its own, has no meaning. It must, that is, submit to a process of interpretation. Each of these processes is, in itself, a mode of creativity. Which is then to say, unavoidably, that at its core – the core of its potentially productive value – psychology is a creative process. An art form. A form of art. Or at least it could be.

12
POIESIS

Does this not bring us back to the poets? Interpretation. The turning of experience into words. This is the act of verse; from Latin *vertere*, 'to turn'. Or perhaps this story was always already the story of poets. From Marko Marulic's first crafting of the term 'psychology', perhaps it ought to have been clear that poetry was going to lie at the heart of any writing of the soul. But what of this poetry? The term 'poetry' comes from the Greek *poiein*, meaning 'to make' or 'to create', but also, 'to build', in the sense of 'to pile up'. As we have seen, verse comes from *vertere*, meaning 'to turn' or 'to transform' but also, in the context of poetry, it relates to the act of ploughing, the turning of the soil creating lines not unlike the lines of poetry on the page. Already, then, in poetry and in verse, we have a double sense of connection to the material, a connection to stone, to earth. A connection to being in the world. In poetry we create, we fashion, we pile up, but pile up what? In verse we turn, we transform, but again, what? The answer which suggests itself here might be 'material', the stuff of the world, the stuff of experience. But again, what we need to keep in mind is that this *stuff* can only ever come to be as experienced through its transformation, through the act of creating which allows it to be accessed. But this is then to say that it is only ever accessed as already transformed.

In trying to access and explain the world around us, tautological as it is, we have no recourse other than to the explanatory framework of the language through which we would already be in the process of making sense of that world. And the same, then, must go for our experience of ourselves. In order to understand, in order to explain, to account for, to describe, in order to *write* the human psyche, we must be poets.

But being a poet here does not mean simply piling up words. Poetry as disengaged repetition says nothing. What passes for poetry in the twenty-first century is often little more than a lackey to institutionalised psychology. Deriving its understanding of the human from an unquestioning ingestion of psychology and retreating into the isolation of the neoliberal individual, this is less writing of the soul than adornment of the ego. Real poetry is always an excess of language, a confrontation with the language that is our *ambience*, a confrontation with the becoming experience in which we find ourselves and thus a confrontation with what we would take ourselves to be and what we would take ourselves to be becoming. Which is then to say that poetry, true poetry, is always already a, or even *the,* mode of the ethical. If we are not but for the confrontation with the question of what we are and language, expression, the struggle of expression, is the only possibility of this confrontation and thus the only possibility of our emerging as subject, then this also implies that this confrontation cannot cease. There is no retreat. No hiding place. This would then also be to say that the responsibility for what we posit ourselves to be and to be becoming, the connections we forge, the communities we become, the pluralities we endorse, at each turn the responsibility sits with no one but me.

We asked once whether universal ethics is feasible, whether it is possible to formulate an ethics which escapes the charge of relativism, whether it is possible for ethics to be anything other than a personal preference or the imposition of one will on another, which would be to say a form of violence. In a sense, we could say, if it is not, then there really is no ethics, only moralities, which we will take or leave depending on our relationship to the creed from which they emerge. The error here is in thinking ethics as distinct and, particularly, as subsequent to the subject. The subject – the one who would be ethical, who would endorse this or that position – arises only in the moment of ethics itself. The two are properly unthinkable apart. It is this, then, that allows us to understand more clearly the absolute nature of the force of the conjunction in the title of this book. Ethics consists in an expression of experience which could never be taken to have been experienced without its subsequent and always inadequate expression. It is this very inadequacy which opens the place for the subject. The subject is what would suture the expression to the always already lost experience. Understood properly as the study of the subject, as the writing of the psyche, which would be the best possible description for this moment, psych-ology would be the discipline of the ethical itself. Understood as an error of statistical application, as an always deceptive cataloguing and containing of normative function, it is hard to see psychology as anything other than an ethical failure.

REFERENCES

APA (American Psychological Association) (2010) *Ethical Principles of Psychologists and Code of Conduct, Including 2010 Amendments*. Available at: http://www.apa.org/ethics/code/index.aspx.

Aristotle (2013 [350 BC]). *The Nichomachean Ethics*. Cambridge: Cambridge University Press.

Bentham, J. (1988 [1776]). *A Fragment on Government*. Cambridge: Cambridge University Press.

Bentham, J. (1996 [1781]). *Introduction to the Principles of Morals and Legislation*. Oxford: Oxford University Press.

Bentham, J. (1988 [1843]). *Anarchical Fallacies: Being A Critical Examination of the Declaration of Rights*. London: William Tait.

Braidotti, R. (2006). *Transpositions*. London: Polity.

BPS (British Psychological Society) (2010). *Code of Human Research Ethics*. Leicester: BPS.

Carver, R. (1981) *What We Talk About When We Talk About Love*. New York: Alfred A. Knopf.

Carver, R. (1989). *A New Path to the Waterfall*. London: Atlantic Books.

Cottingham, J. (1998). *Philosophy and the Good Life*. Cambridge: Cambridge University Press.

Darley, J.M. and Latané, B. (1968). 'Bystander intervention in emergencies: Diffusion of responsibility'. *Journal of Personality and Social Psychology*, 8: 377–83.

Derrida, J. (1999). *Adieu to Emmanuel Levinas*. Stanford, CA: Stanford University Press.

Eysenck, H.J. (1971). *Race, Intelligence, Education*. London: Maurice Temple.

Freud, S. (1923). 'The ego and the id'. In J. Strachey (ed. and trans.), *The Standard Edition of the Complete Psychological Works of Sigmund Freud*, (Vol. 19, pp. 3–66). London: Hogarth Press.

Gansberg, M. (1964). 'New York woman killed while witnesses do nothing'. *New York Times*, 26 March.

Haney, C., Banks, C., and Zimbardo, P.G. (1973). 'Interpersonal dynamics in a simulated prison'. *International Journal of Criminology and Penology*, 1: 69–97.

Hume, D. (2003 [1739]). *A Treatise of Human Nature*. Mineola, NY: Dover Publications.

Kafka, F. (2007 [1925]). *The Trial*. London: Penguin.

Kant, I. (1993 [1785]). *Grounding for the Metaphysics of Morals*. Indianapolis, IN: Hackett.

Kant, I. (2003 [1787]). *Critique of Pure Reason*. Basingstoke: Palgrave Macmillan.

Kant, I. (1997 [1788]). *Critique of Practical Reason*. Cambridge: Cambridge University Press.

Kant, I. (1987 [1790]). *Critique of Judgement*. Indianapolis, IN: Hackett.

Kant, I. (1993 [1797]). 'On A Supposed Right to Lie Because of Philanthropic Concerns'. In *Grounding for the Metaphysics of Morals*. Indianapolis, IN: Hackett.

Kant, I. (1997). *Lectures on Ethics*. Cambridge: Cambridge University Press.

Keats, J. (2009). *Selected Letters*. Oxford: Oxford University Press.

Krstic, K. (1964). 'Marko Marulic: The author of the term psychology'. *Acta Instituti Psychologici Universitatis Zagrabiensis*, 36: 7–13.

Latané, B. and Rodin, J. (1969). 'A lady in distress: Inhibiting effects of friends and strangers on bystander intervention'. *Journal of Experimental Social Psychology*, 5: 189–202.

Lyotard, J. (1979). *The Post-modern Condition*. Manchester: Manchester University Press.

Metzinger, T. (2003). *Being No One: The Self-Model Theory of Subjectivity*. Cambridge, MA: MIT Press.

Milgram, S. (1963). 'Behavioural study of obedience'. *The Journal of Abnormal and Social Psychology*, 67(4): 371–8.

Milgram, S. (1974). *Obedience to Authority: An Experimental View*. London: Pinter & Martin.

Mill, J.S. (1991 [1859]). 'On Liberty'. In *On Liberty and other Essays*. Oxford: Oxford University Press.

Mill, J.S. (1991 [1861]). 'Utilitarianism'. In *On Liberty and other Essays*. Oxford: Oxford University Press.

Moore, G.E. (1903). *Principia Ethica*. Cambridge: Cambridge University Press.

Nietzsche, F. (2002 [1882]). *The Gay Science*. Cambridge: Cambridge University Press.

Nietzsche, F. (2002 [1886]). *Beyond Good and Evil*. Cambridge: Cambridge University Press.

Paley, W. (1815). *The Principles of Moral and Political Philosophy*. London: West & Richardson.

Piliavin, I.M., Rodin, J.A. and Piliavin, J. (1969). 'Good Samaritanism: An underground phenomenon?'. *Journal of Personality and Social Psychology*, 13: 289–99.

Raspe, R.E. (2012 [1785]). *The Surprising Adventures of Baron Münchausen*. New York: Melville House.

Schreber, D.P. (2000 [1903]). *Memoir of My Nervous Illness*. New York: New York Review Books.

Warburton, N. (2014). *Philosophy: The classics*. London: Routledge.

Zlotnick, A. and Mukhopadhyay, S. (2011) 'Virus assembly, allostery and antivirals'. *Trends in Microbiology*, 19(1) 14–23.

Film and television

Birdman (2014). Directed by Alejandro González Iñárritu. USA. Fox Searchlight Pictures.

The Heist (2006). Presented by Derren Brown. UK. Channel 4.

The Omen (1976). Directed by Richard Donner. USA/UK. 20th Century Fox.

Sátántangó (1994). Directed by Béla Tarr. Hungary. Artificial Eye.

We Need to Talk About Kevin (2011). Directed by Lynne Ramsay. USA/UK. Artificial Eye.

INDEX

Taylor & Francis eBooks

Helping you to choose the right eBooks for your Library

Add Routledge titles to your library's digital collection today. Taylor and Francis ebooks contains over 50,000 titles in the Humanities, Social Sciences, Behavioural Sciences, Built Environment and Law.

Choose from a range of subject packages or create your own!

Benefits for you
- » Free MARC records
- » COUNTER-compliant usage statistics
- » Flexible purchase and pricing options
- » All titles DRM-free.

Benefits for your user
- » Off-site, anytime access via Athens or referring URL
- » Print or copy pages or chapters
- » Full content search
- » Bookmark, highlight and annotate text
- » Access to thousands of pages of quality research at the click of a button.

REQUEST YOUR **FREE** INSTITUTIONAL TRIAL TODAY | **Free Trials Available**
We offer free trials to qualifying academic, corporate and government customers.

eCollections – Choose from over 30 subject eCollections, including:

Archaeology	Language Learning
Architecture	Law
Asian Studies	Literature
Business & Management	Media & Communication
Classical Studies	Middle East Studies
Construction	Music
Creative & Media Arts	Philosophy
Criminology & Criminal Justice	Planning
Economics	Politics
Education	Psychology & Mental Health
Energy	Religion
Engineering	Security
English Language & Linguistics	Social Work
Environment & Sustainability	Sociology
Geography	Sport
Health Studies	Theatre & Performance
History	Tourism, Hospitality & Events

For more information, pricing enquiries or to order a free trial, please contact your local sales team:
www.tandfebooks.com/page/sales